JOHN WESLEY and the AMERICAN FRONTIER

John Fremont Beeson

xulon PRESS

To Eva

PREFACE

The title of this book, *John Wesley and the American Frontier*, is a little misleading, quite misleading actually. John Wesley was never on what we think of as the American Frontier. He never rode west on the seat of a covered wagon. He never fought hostile Indians. He never hunted for his food with a long rifle. He never built a log cabin or a sod house. In fact there is real humor in trying to imagine the little English gentlemen, Oxford Don, Fellow of Lincoln College in his clerical garb, in that setting. It can be accurately said, however, that Wesley was on the American frontier when the original thirteen colonies were the frontier. He spent 1737 and parts of 1736 and 1738 in Georgia Colony.

The Rev. Mr. John Wesley, M.A. did not move west with the intrepid pioneers. What did go west with them was Wesley's theology. It is the contention of this book that the theology that went west with the pioneers was a somewhat mangled version of Wesley's theology. The purpose of this book is to ascertain what changes did take place in the theology of John Wesley on the American frontier in the nineteenth century and to determine what influences impacted on that theology to bring about those changes. That something did happen to Wesley's High Church, Anglican theology on the American Frontier would seem quite evident to even the casual observer. The author deems it important that we know what changes took place, what factors of frontier life impacted on Wesley's theology to bring about those changes, and what those changes mean to us as we strive for renewal in our churches. It is the author's belief that a return to Wesley's theology rather than a return to Wesley's theology as it was understood on the American frontier might be of more value to us as we seek church renewal in the twenty-first century.

I would like to express my appreciation to my friends, The Rev. Victor Metivier and The Rev. Chuck Excell who read parts of the manuscript and commented on it. I would like also to express my appreciation to Maureen Park for keyboarding the manuscript, and for her patience through its many changes. I would especially like to express my appreciation to my wife, Eva, to whom this book is dedicated for her many years of love and support.

TABLE OF CONTENTS

CHAPTER ONE:
INTRODUCTION

It seems appropriate to begin our study with a brief sketch of John Wesley's time in Georgia. This is important for our purposes because it was during and just after his time in Georgia that Wesley passed through a period of turmoil, "the soul's dark night" in which he had serious doubts concerning his relationship to God and grave fears concerning his personal salvation. During his time in Georgia and for a year or so after, he was exposed to the Moravians, a German pietist group, who led him to believe that he was misguided in seeking his personal salvation through the means of grace, including the sacraments, and through reason rather than through simple faith alone. The Moravians convinced Wesley that his lack of assurance concerning his salvation was the direct result of his lack of faith. It was out of this period of spiritual turmoil, under the guidance of the Moravians, that

Wesley came into his "heart warming" experience and began developing his own theology, which was to be a balance between faith and works and between faith and reason.

The twenty-one months that Wesley spent in Georgia were without a doubt the most turbulent period of his life. By disposition, by training, by his religious mindset, he was totally unsuited for the work he went to Georgia to perform, that of being parish priest and missionary to the Indians. Wesley's personal dream of converting the "heathen Indians" to Christianity was thwarted because Governor Oglethorpe saw it as far to dangerous and because he needed Wesley for the work for which he had brought him to Georgia, that of parish priest.

During his time in Georgia John Wesley was still in his religious prig phase. The dictionary definition of prig is as follows: "b. a person who is excessively precise, proper and smug in his moral behavior and attitudes, to the annoyance of others"[1]. This definition perfectly describes John Wesley, the thirty two year old Anglican priest in Georgia.

Unfortunately Wesley, as a parish priest, in Savannah and nearby Frederica, was not content with being a religious prig on his own, but sought rather, to impose his beliefs and practices on his parishioners. It was his insistence that his parishioners live as he lived that got him in trouble with the very patient Governor Oglethorpe and not so patient citizens of Savannah and the near by villages, and was one of the contributing factors to his failure in Georgia.

Shortly after arriving in Georgia, Wesley wrote in his Sunday, 9 May 1736 journal entry, "I began dividing public prayer, according to the original appointment of The Church of England (still observed in a few places in England). The morning service began at five; the Communion Office at eleven; the Evening Service at three; this day I began prayers in the court house, a large and convenient place[2].

This scheduling of Sunday Services was not done for the convenience of the parishioners, that they might choose the service that best fit their schedules. Wesley expected them to be present at all three services. He openly reprimanded those who did not comply and in some instances refused them the sacrament of Holy Communion. An interesting phrase in the above quote from Wesley is that which appears in parenthesis (Wesley's parenthesis) indicating that the schedule of Sunday Services being imposed on the busy pioneers, building houses, clearing land and establishing themselves in trades and business, had been out of vogue in England for some time. It is not difficult to see why this imposed schedule was the source of some resentment toward Wesley. To further add to the resentment, Wesley persuaded Governor Oglethorpe to ban hunting and fishing on Sundays.

Wesley's journal entry for the next day, Monday, 10 May 1736 says, "I began visiting my parishioners in order, from house to house; for which I set apart (the time they could not work because of the heat, viz.) from twelve to three in the afternoon."[3]. We can assume these visits in the middle of the day, when they were resting from hard labor in the intense heat, were not a source of joy for his parishioners. They were not likely brief visits for the purpose of getting acquainted, but were probably rather lengthy visits during which Wesley inquired as to the spiritual condition of the various family members.

Another example of Wesley's religious intransigence is found in his Journal entry of 5 May 1736, "I was asked to baptize a child of Mr. Parker's, Second Bailiff of Savannah; but Mrs. Parker told me, "Neither Mr. Parker, nor I will consent to its being dipped." I answered, "If you certify that the child is weak, it will suffice." (The rubric says) "To pour water upon it." She replied, "Nay, the child is not weak; but I am resolved it shall not be dipped." This argument I could not refute. So I went home; and the child was baptized by another person."[4]. There were at least two other priests in the Savannah area at the time, including a military chaplain.

Another problem Wesley had in Georgia was that in his role as their spiritual leader he got himself embroiled in the petty disagreements and gossip of the people, especially the women.

Through out his life Wesley's relationships with women were problematic and somewhat strange. The reason for this would be the work of a psychiatrist and not pertinent to what we are attempting in this book. Through out his life Wesley was attracted to women and apparently some women found him attractive as well. Wesley, however, seemed incapable of making a real commitment though he came close a few times. He did marry a widow later in life, but it was far from a model marriage and they ended up living separately. He missed her funeral!

One of the times he came close to making a commitment to a relationship with a young woman occurred during his brief stay in Georgia. Sophy Hopkey, an attractive young woman of sixteen or seventeen, (half his age) in the care of her uncle, a Mr. Causton, caught Wesley's attention. He spent a great deal of time with her in giving her religious instruction and in teaching her French grammar. This seems a strange way to woo a young woman! Other topics must have been discussed, for Wesley led Sophy to believe that he might be interested in her in other ways than as a pupil. As always in these matters, Wesley played along the edge but could not move into the deeper waters of commitment. He found himself sexually attracted to Sophy but believing these desires to be incompatible with his spiritual goals he wrestled mightily with himself.

Sophy eventually tired of the game and married a Mr. William Williamson. In his Journal entry for 3 July 1737, referring to Sophy, Wesley wrote, "Immediately after Holy Communion, I mentioned to Mrs. Williamson (Mr. Causton's niece) some things I thought reprovable in her behavior. At this she appeared extremely angry; she said she did not expect such usage from me; and at the turn of the street, through which we were passing on our way home, went abruptly away."[5].

Wesley further incurred the wrath of Sophy and her husband, Mr. Williamson, and their families and friends, by turning Sophy away from Holy

Communion. The reason he gave was that she had not stated her intention to receive Communion on the previous day, as technically she should have done. Could it be that the use of that technicality on this occasion had more to do with pique on Wesley's part than it had to do with a defense of the Church's rubric?

Finally the citizens of the Georgia Colony had all they could take of their overbearing young priest. On 1 September 1737 a Grand Jury handed down a list of grievances against John Wesley for which he was to be tried. The first two had to do with Sophy, "By speaking and writing to Mrs. Williamson against her husband's consent and by repelling her from Holy Communion."[6]. Rather than facing the charges, Wesley fled Georgia for the Carolinas where he took a ship back to England in early December 1737, thus becoming a fugitive from the law!

Years later, on 10 September 1784, following the successful conclusion of the American Revolutionary War, Wesley sent the American Methodists a worship book titled, The Sunday Service of the Methodist in North America. These books were printed in London but were not bound there. They were to be bound in America to avoid a tax on bound books. A letter to "Dr. Coke, Mr. Asbury, and our brethren in North America" came with the unbound worship books. The first sentence in that letter said, "By a very uncommon train of providence, many of the provinces of North America are totally disjoined from their mother country, and erected into independent states."[7]. This sentence is significant in that it indicates

Wesley's disbelief that God would allow such a thing to happen, and that if God had not made a mistake it was at least beyond Wesley's understanding. In that same letter, as a reason for sending the book, Wesley wrote of "feeding the poor sheep in the wilderness."[8]. It can only be imagined what the citizens of Boston, New York, Philadelphia and Baltimore thought about being described as poor sheep in the wilderness. The last sentence in that letter again expresses Wesley's disbelief that God would allow the Americans to separate from England. The lengthy sentence reads, "As our American brethren are now totally disentangled both from the state and the English Hierarchy, we dare not entangle them again, either with one or the other. They are now at full liberty, simply to follow the primitive church. As we judge it best that they should stand fast in that liberty, with which God has so strangely made them free."[9]. As can be seen from this sentence, John Wesley never really reconciled to there being a United States of America. John Wesley was never Americanized. What was Americanized on the American frontier was Wesley's theology; Americanized, in some instances, to the point Wesley might have had difficulty in recognizing it as his own. An examination of the scope of those changes and the factors that contributed to those changes is the purpose of this book.

After his Aldersgate "conversion" on 24 May 1738, which he described as, "I felt my heart strangely warmed" the eighteenth century English clergyman, The Rev. John Wesley, M.A. began a renewal movement within the Church of England.

The movement was organized into an ever growing number of groups or societies for study, prayer and spiritual formation. The people in these societies were called Methodists by their detractors because of the methodical way in which they organized their lives to make time for all their religious activities. The name Methodists was first used against Wesley and his little group of fellow students who composed the Holy Club at Oxford, and who practiced a very organized and structured life style so as to make time for their religious practices.

His Aldersgate experience made such an impression on Wesley that he boldly claimed he had not been a Christian before that experience. This caused a great deal of consternation among his friends and followers who knew him, before Aldersgate, to have been a highly religious person, spending much time in study, prayer and in doing good. Wesley, himself, in later life expressed the feeling that he had put too much emphasis on the Aldersgate experience in his spiritual journey. It needs to be remembered here that at the time of his Aldersgate experience Wesley was still very much under the influence of the Moravians who saw the Aldersgate type experience, a total reliance on faith for salvation, to be the totality of Christian experience. Wesley was soon to part company with the Moravians over this point. He saw the means of grace to be of great value in the Christian's growth towards a more holy life. Also, Wesley would agree with St. James, that, "Faith without works is dead".

John Wesley lived and died a fairly High Church Anglican priest. During his lifetime Wesley was able to keep the Methodists from breaking with the Church of England. Upon his death, however, the English Methodists did break with the Church of England. Before Wesley's death, following the successful outcome of the American Revolutionary War, the Methodists in America, now left on their own, formed a new church, The Methodist Episcopal Church in North America. Though John Wesley was not a systematic theologian, that is he did not set down a system of theology, doctrine by doctrine, he did develop a theology, or at least a theological emphasis, which he believed to be very little, if at all different from that of the Church of England. This theology was put forth in his sermons, his notes on the Old and New Testaments, and in other writings and to some extend, in the hymns of early Methodism. The majority of those hymns were written by his brother, Charles, who was also an Anglican priest and very much involved with John in the Methodist Societies.

Later in this book we will contend that there were other than Anglican roots to Wesley's theology, and we will explore those roots. It seems possible that Wesley was not aware of those other roots. As he progressed to his mature theological understanding he continued to believe wholeheartedly that his theology was not different from that of the Church of England.

The purpose of this book is to examine what, if anything happened to John Wesley's theology on the

American frontier between 1784, when the United States of America became a nation, and 1884 when the American frontier was drawing to a close.

The American Methodists established the Methodist Episcopal Church independent of the Church of England in the same year, 1784, that the nation was established independent of England. During the next one hundred years Methodism became the largest and fastest growing religious movement in the country and exerted a real civilizing influence on the frontier as it moved ever west.

The contention of this book is that Wesley's theology underwent a dramatic evolution on the American frontier that left it much changed. The differences between Wesley's theology and its Americanized version can most clearly be seen in the Wesleyan doctrines of Grace and Christian perfection. We will examine four factors of the American frontier that impacted on Wesley's theology to bring about its Americanization. Those factors were: First, An uneducated clergy; Second, A plurality of religious groups in America; Third, The American mind set on the frontier (anti-authoritarian, rugged individualism); Fourth, Revivalism and the camp meeting movement.

The existence of several smaller Methodist churches that broke off from the Methodist Episcopal Church during the nineteenth century, each claiming to be the group adhering to Wesley's theology, would indicate that there was not a common understanding of Wesley's theology in nineteenth century America. It must be noted in fairness, however, that not all the breaks with the Methodist Episcopal Church were for doctrinal reasons, though most made that claim. Some involved polity, as in the case of the Methodist Protestant Church; some involved political consid- erations, as in the case of the Methodist Episcopal Church South; and though it would be vociferously denied, some involved personality clashes, big egos colliding. These clashes were always couched in doctrinal terms!

For these smaller churches rooted in Wesley theology, the maintenance of that theology, as it was understood and practiced on the American frontier, was their reason for being. The question is, were they faithful to the theology of John Wesley or were they faithful to the somewhat mangled version of Wesley's theology as it came to be understood and practiced on the American frontier? The author contends that it was to the latter to which they were faithful, and that Wesley might have been very uncomfortable with some of it. To put it another way, if one could have put the Rev. John Wesley, M.A., the Oxford don, fellow of Lincoln College in the same room with Peter Cartwright, the archetype of the American circuit riding preacher and left them there for a while, they would both have been uncomfortable, would not have had much to talk about and would not have agreed on a lot of things. They probably would not really have liked each other.

One of the major points on which they would have differed would have been their view concerning the education of clergy. Peter Cartwright in the preface to his autobiography, writing about the early circuit riding preachers of the frontier says, "But it must be remembered that many of us early traveling preachers, who entered the vast wilderness of the west at an early day, had little or no education; no books, and no time to read them if we could have had them".[9] John Wesley in England, on the other hand, in giving advice to his lay preachers, instructed them to spend the morning hours from six to twelve, with an hour out for breakfast, in reading and studying. To those who said, "But I have no taste for reading." Wesley replied, "Contract a taste for it by use, or return to your trade."[10].

Wesley was successful in evangelizing England, and Cartwright and his kind were very successful in evangelizing the American frontier. But they were not interchangeable! Wesley would have been unintelligible to the people to whom Cartwright preached as would Cartwright have been to the people to whom Wesley preached.

From what each wrote about the other's type it would seem that they might have had some contempt for the other's type. And, yet, Cartwright, and the circuit riding preachers he represented, believed themselves to have been true followers of John Wesley and true to his doctrines. Their fervor and dedication cannot be questioned, nor their success in evangelizing the frontier. This author, however, believes them to have been wrong in their belief that they were true to Wesley's theology.

Sydney E. Ahlstrom, writing in his book, A Religious History of the American People, concerning an Evangelist named Potter Jones, who was active in The Methodist Episcopal Church South right after the Civil War, says, "No man documented so tellingly the long road away from John Wesley's theology which American Methodism had traveled in its first century of independent life." To support this assertion, Ahlstrom quotes Jones as saying; "If I had a creed I would sell it to a museum." Says Ahlstrom of Jones, "Sanctification he equated with a resolve to live by the mores of rural Georgia in the wicket city."[11]. Jones came close to the end of the time period with which we are dealing (1784-1874). As Ahlstrom pointed out, Jones demonstrated the vast difference between Wesley's theology and what passed for Wesley's theology in nineteenth century America.

As has been stated following the successful conclusion of the American Revolution, a fact to which Wesley never quite reconciled, he sent a worship book to the American Methodist, The Sunday Service of the Methodists in North America. In his brief introduction to that book he wrote, "I believe there is no Liturgy in the world, either in ancient or modern language, which breathes more solid scriptural, rational piety than the Book of Common Prayer of the Church of England.... Little alteration is made in the following edition of it, which I recommend to our societies in America, except in the following instances..."[12]. Though Wesley claimed little alteration of the Book of Common Prayer, an examination shows more than a little alteration, especially in the Articles of Religion. He sent twenty-five of the original thirty-nine to America and some of these he altered. He left out several psalms as unfit for Christian lips. However, the book was close enough to the Book of Common Prayer, that had it been extensively used, it would have made the Methodist Episcopal Church very similar to the Church of England. That American Methodism developed into something quite different than Wesley had invisioned seems evident.

In the following chapters we will seek to understand the extent to which American Methodist theology on the frontier deviated from John Wesley's theology and how and why that deviation came to be.

These questions are deemed important to church renewal. Why? Because when we speak of returning to our roots for guidance in the twenty-first century we need to be very clear as to which roots we are returning, those of the Anglican scholar/evangelist grounded in catholic theology (catholic with a small c) or to what came to be considered Wesley's theology in the anti-intellectual and emotionally charged climate of the American frontier. It is important that we know. Why? Because it is just possible that John Wesley, properly understood, might be of more value to a renewal of American Methodism in our time than a return to that which was incorrectly understood to be Wesley's theology on the frontier over a century ago. Much of the revivalism of the nineteenth and twentieth century was urging a return to the frontier faith as the "old time religion".

The frontier is long gone and the mindset of the frontier is fast fading from the American psyche. It's possible Wesley speaks more authentically to our present situation than does Wesley as understood on the American frontier.

The task before us, then, seems obvious, to understand the extent and direction of deviation from Wesley's theology. To do that demands that we have a least a cursory understanding of Wesley's theology. That is a challenge. There are several problems in discovering just what Wesley's mature and final judgements were on particular doctrines. A great many books have been written on Wesley's theology. There is much disagreement. People have tended to find in Wesley what they need to support their own views. The First problem in understanding Wesley's theology was Wesley's unwillingness or inability to see that he did, indeed, at some points disagree with the teachings of the Church of England or at least that he had a very different way of looking at some of those teachings. When asked at what point he differed with the doctrines of that church, he invariably responded, that to the best of his knowledge he differed not at all. We can be sure that was an honest answer from his perspective, but others have not been so sure of its accuracy.

The Second problem in coming to an understanding of Wesley's theology is the vast quantity of his writings over a period of sixty plus years. It is a daunting task to gather his thoughts on any one subject. He was not a systematic theologian!

Third, is Wesley's intellectual honesty. He freely admitted to having changed his mind on some matters and to having had doubts about others. When pressed to say what Wesley said on a particular subject, one must ask, when? The revivalist, the fundamentalist, the social action people, those with high sacramental leanings, all can find in Wesley's writings what they want. How often we hear, "O but Wesley said..."

The Fourth problem in understanding Wesley's theology is, as has been stated, he was not a systematic theologian. That is not to say there is not a consistency or direction in Wesley's theology. It is simply to say that he wrote no system of theology to which we can go for what he taught on specific doctrines. Rather we must sort through over sixty years of his writings, his sermons, his notes on the Old and New Testaments, his pamphlets and books. It is indeed a daunting task. Fortunately many people have devoted many years to the task, and though they don't always agree, we can lean on their scholarship as we move forward.

Before leaving this chapter we probably need to make sure we are in agreement as to whether or not the United Methodist Church early in the twenty-first century needs renewal. It seems impossible that any thoughtful, informed person could question the need for renewal in the United Methodist Church. A church that has declined steadily in membership for 40 years, from its high water mark of 11,050,634 in 1964 to 8,300,000 in 2006 would seem to need renewal. This is especially true when one considers that church was once the largest and fastest growing church in the nation and that during that 40 years of steady decline there was a merger with another church, The Evangelical United Brethren that brought in several hundred thousand members. During those 40 years of decline a good year was one in which the rate of decline was less than that of the previous year.

There are several reasons for this dramatic decline. For the purposes of this study we will suggest only one of those reasons. That reason is the lack of any consensus concerning doctrinal matters. In 1972 the General Conference said, "Theological pluralism should be recognized as a principle." In reality this was simply a statement of the fact that we were already operating on that basis. Any mention of theological pluralism was later removed, but the fact of theological pluralism has continued. One outcome of theological pluralism is that creeds are almost never used in our worship. Creeds assume a certain theological agreement.

Pluralism would be perfectly acceptable in a search for truth in a university philosophy department but in a theological seminary of a church founded on the sound doctrines of John Wesley or for that matter, the basic doctrines of historic Christianity, it is treasonable. On one occasion when this author was riding to a cabinet meeting with another and much younger superintendent, that superintendent asked, "Why shouldn't I believe in reincarnation?" Why not indeed, it fits into the broad spectrum of theological pluralism. That's not the answer I gave, but the question does indicate the grave dangers in theological pluralism. A church that cannot stand together and affirm a faith about which there is some consensus is a church in a dangerous drift. The ship has lost its rudder and is in danger of foundering. This author's conclusion is that The United Methodist Church, along with the rest of the "main line" churches needs renewal.

CHAPTER TWO: THE DIVERSE ROOTS OF WESLEY'S THEOLOGY

As with all theologians, so it was with John Wesley, his mature theological thought was molded by his own life experiences as well as by his study of the writings of other theologians. In Wesley's case this study included the Early Church Fathers, Roman Catholic and Anglican mystics as well as secular literary classics. Wesley was a very capable linguist and read the scriptures daily in their original languages. For Wesley study was a life long pursuit. He set aside several hours a day for study. He said that when he traveled on horseback he gave the horse its head (allowed the horse to pick the path) so he could spend some time reading. That must have been some horse!

The temptation is strong to place considerably more importance on Wesley's life experiences than on his extensive study in the formation of his mature theology. That John Wesley was the son of Samuel and Susanna Wesley, and that his upbringing in that parsonage home impacted strongly on his religious thinking cannot be denied. But that does not fully account for where Wesley ended up in his theological thinking.

It has been established that Wesley was not a systematic theologian. To hammer out a coherent system of theology was not Wesley's aim. One cannot help wishing, at times, that he had set down a system of theology, doctrine by doctrine, to which one might go for edification on specific doctrines. But that was not to be.

There are at least two reasons why Wesley did not hammer out a systematic theology. First, to compile a systematic theology occupies a great portion of one's life. Wesley was busy fanning the flames of a great evangelical revival in which he played a predominant role.

Second, in contrast to the assurance with which Wesley usually wrote and preached, his thoughts were in a state of flux and growth through out his life.

Wesley was a pragmatist. What worked to keep the revival alive and vital had to be true. There is a legitimate question as to whether Wesley's theology molded the revival or the revival molded Wesley's theology. It was probably some of both. Wesley freely admitted, to having changed his mind on some matters after further study, conversation and experience.

Wesley's purpose in life was to bring a "heart warming" religious experience to the English speaking world through a renewal of his beloved Church of England. Theology for Wesley was not an end itself, rather a means to an end. That end being the evangelization of the British Isles and England's colonies.

His theology was thus eclectic and pragmatic. Its purpose was to explain, and to continue an observable phenomenon, the Wesleyan revival in English society.

The common complaint about theologians is that theologians write to be read by other theologians, thus are unintelligible to the rest of us. That charge cannot be leveled against Wesley. His sermons and writings were meant for people who had no theological learning. Albert Outler, in his book, *John Wesley,* writes:

> For all this borrowing and mixing under pressure and heat of a great popular movement, Wesley's theology emerges clear and consistent and integral. It is at this level that a claim to originality may be registered for him – and tested. Many other theological systems are bolder, subtler, and more massive – but none has more intense and sustained evangelical concern. He seems to have been aware that the strength of his position lay in its simple profundity, and this prompted him to make frequent summaries of it – usually with a clear drawn boundary line between doctrine

> and "opinion". This makes for a certain repe-
> titiousness – and yet also a certain cumula-
> tive impact of his thought upon the attentive
> reader. [1]

There are three pertinent points in the above quote from Outler. First, the end result of Wesley's theologizing was a clear, consistent and integral theology. Second, it fit with Wesley's goal of explaining and sustaining the evangelical revival that was in process at that time in England. Third, Wesley was very aware of the distinction between essential doctrines and religious opinion. Through out his entire life Wesley staunchly defended what he considered essential doctrines, and they were surprisingly few, while being at times tolerant and at times indifferent to religious opinions that differed from his. Wesley wrote in his, *A Further Appeal to Men of Reason and Religion*, in answer to the criticism of some against the doctrines he taught:

> I will briefly mention what those doctrines
> are, before I consider the objections to them.
> Now, all I teach respects either the nature and
> condition of justification and saving faith, or
> the author of faith and salvation.[2]

Wesley's theological views were not easily arrived at, nor did they ever become static. At nearly the end of his long life he was rephrasing, refining and in some cases retracting some of his earlier writings. We will deal with this in a latter chapter.

ROOTS AMONG THE DISSENTERS:

Wesley always considered himself, and for the most part was, a high church Anglican. There can be no question, however, that some of his theological emphasis had their root in the soil of the dissenters. His mother Susanna, though staunchly Church of England, came from a dissenting family. She was the daughter of Dr. Samuel Annesley, a prominent dissenting clergyman. In his journal entry for 3 September 1739, Wesley wrote of a conversation he had with his mother concerning the religious experience of her father, Dr, Annesley. In that conversation, his mother assured him that her father had enjoyed the assurance of his sins forgiven, and that he expressed this shortly before his death, though she had no recollection of his ever having preached it as a possibility for others.[3]

In spite of the fact that Wesley considered himself a high church Anglican, recognizing that as his heritage, some of his practices such as extemporaneous prayer, field preaching, and the use of unordained preachers, and the ordination by Wesley of some of his lay preachers for the American Methodists, indicated a theology of church, that at some points was more akin to that of the dissenters than to the Church of England. Susanna who, though she converted to Anglicanism at the age of fifteen, apparently with her father, Dr. Annesley's blessing, at least over no strong objections, retained some of her dissenting views concerning the church. In the absence of her husband, Samuel, from his pulpit in Epworth, it was Susanna who conducted services in the rectory with attendance approaching two hundred, while her husband's curate conducted services in the church for a sparse congregation. She excused herself to her husband upon his return on the basis that what she had done was not preaching but Bible study since she had not taken a text. As Wesley made use of lay – preachers and allowed women to speak in and even conduct meetings among the women in his societies, he was to make good use of this fine piece of rationalization of his mother's which said that if a text was not used it was not preaching.

It was Susanna, when Wesley was horrified to learn that one of his lay preachers had administered the sacrament of Holy Communion, who said that she had heard the young man preach and that she was satisfied that he was as fully called to God to be a minister as her son. This was certainly more the view of a dissenter than that of an Anglican!

Susanna may have converted to Anglicanism but in many ways her free spirit was not converted and she retained strong dissenting tendencies in her religion, which she passed on to her son John. Whenever Wesley found his Puritan (dissenting) roots and his Anglican roots to be in conflict, it was Susanna who helped him to rationalize in favor of Puritanism. Robert G. Tuttle, Jr. in his book, *John Wesley, His Life and his Theology*, finds an even more subtle influence on Wesley. There were two conflicting schools of thought prevalent in religion in eighteenth century England. This conflict was most pronounced in Puritanism. This conflict triggered a corresponding conflict in Wesley prior to Aldersgate and from which he was never quite free even after Aldersgate.

Tuttle points out that "The early eighteenth century was a breeding ground for theological schizophrenia." There were two distinct and conflicting schools of thought, one the Aristotelian model and the other the Platonic model.

The Aristotelian model's use in theological thought led to the conclusion that reason leads to faith. Tuttle states that the Arminianism of the Church of England, which saw the human heart, but not the mind corrupted, left room for the Aristotelian model in Anglican theology. Tuttle goes on to say:

> To a lesser extent, one branch of Puritanism followed the same model. The Puritan appeal to reason was to use logic as a goal to make thought clear, although faith (as in Church of England) was a matter of divine revelation (where God completes the natural theology not observable in nature alone) the intellect through practical theology sought to maneuver the heart into disposition of faith.[4]

That is simply to say, reason leads to faith.

Tuttle continues with a definition of the Platonic model as appropriated in theology.

The second school of thought included (those who use the Platonic model) who thought that reality had to do with ideas. Matter, though perceivable by sense experience, was an illusion. Since reality had to do with ideas, not sense experience, understanding came (deductively) by faith. In a phrase – faith leads to reason.[5]

The Platonic model is compatible with certain strains of mysticism, though the more radical mystics would bypass both faith and reason for direct access to God through a kind of absorption. It is obvious that one cannot use both the Aristotelian and Platonic models at the same time. Tuttle finds still another strain in the Puritanism of Wesley's time, those who, with the evangelicals, found both the human heart and the intellect corrupted, and who believed that only the grace of God, drawing us by faith would lead us to understanding (salvation).

The result of schizophrenia in religion in Wesley's day between two conflicting schools of thought, the Aristotelian and the Platonic, can be seen in the Puritan reaction to Quakers on the one hand and to the Anglicans on the other.

In his early religious life Wesley struggled with trying to reconcile the two irreconcilable schools of thought. It seems safe to say that Wesley's "first conversion" in 1725 at the time of his ordination as a deacon in the Church of England was after the Aristotelian model and that his Aldersgate "conversion" in 1738 was after the Platonic model. Both conversions were to play important roles in his mature theological thought.

ANGLICAN ROOTS:

Did John Wesley's theology differ from that of the Church of England? If one were forced to answer that question with one word, the answer would have to be yes. Yes, inspite of Wesley's testimony to the contrary. From his Aldersgate conversion in May of 1738 until his death in 1791 Wesley always maintained that he was in full theological agreement with the Church of England; that his doctrines were her doctrines. In his journal entry for 13 September 1739 he wrote as follows:

> A serious clergyman desired to know in what points we (Methodists) differ from the Church of England. I answered, "to the best of my knowledge, in none. The doctrines that we preach are the doctrines of the Church of England, indeed the fundamental doctrines of the Church, clearly laid down in her Prayers, Articles and Homilies." He then asked," At what points, then, do you differ from the other clergy of the Church of England?" I answered, "In none from that part of the clergy who adhere to the doctrines of the church; but from the part of the Clergy who dissent from the Church (though they own it not,) I differ in the points following:

Wesley then listed five points in which he differed, not with the Church of England, but with those clergymen who, according to Wesley, were the real dissenters, being untrue to the doctrines of that Church.

Again Wesley wrote in his journal entry for 6 February 1740:

> I think it was the next time that I was there. (Newgate Prison) that the Ordinary (bishop) of Newgate came to me, and with much vehemence told me, that he was sorry that I should turn dissenter from the Church of England. I told him, if it was so, I did not know it: At which he seemed surprised; and offered at something by way of proof, but which needed not a reply.[6]

Another quote shows how firmly Wesley saw himself to be within the Church of England.

> Our twentieth Article defines a true Church as a congregation of faithful people, wherein the true word of God is preached, and the sacraments duly administered. Who then are the worst dissenters from the Church?[7]

Wesley, then, went on to answer that rhetorical question with: "-people who do all sorts of "sinful things", some of which he listed, and "those who teach false doctrine."[8]

It can be noted that the above quotes from Wesley, concerning his faithfulness to the doctrines of the Church of England, came within a year or two of his Aldersgate experience. One might gather from that fact that circumstances later caused Wesley to revise his views concerning the doctrines of the Church of England. That does not seem to be the case. One more quote from Wesley's journal, the entry for 12 April 1789 (being Easter Sunday) nearly fifty years after his Aldersgate conversion and within two years of his death, suffices to show that Wesley's views concerning the Church of England did not change throughout his life. Wesley believed himself to have been faithful to the doctrines of the Church of England at the end of his long life and ministry as he was at the beginning of his ministry. In that journal entry for 12 April 1789 Wesley wrote:

> Afterwards I met the society, and explained to them at large the original design of the Methodists, viz. not to be a distinct party, but to stir up all parties, Christian or heathen, to worship God in Spirit and in truth but the Church of England in particular; to which they belonged from the beginning. With this view, I have uniformly gone on for fifty years, never varying from the doctrines of the Church at all; not from her disciplines, of choice but of necessity: so in a course of years, necessity was laid on me, (as I have proved elsewhere,) 1. To preach in the open air. 2. To pray extempore. 3. To form societies. 4. To accept the assistance of lay preachers: and in a few other instances, to use such means as occurred, to prevent or remove evils that we either felt or feared.[9]

When one learns that one of the "means that occurred in a few other instances" was the ordination of clergy by Wesley for the work in America, though Wesley was not a bishop and was in an episcopal church in which only bishops ordained, one is inclined to question Wesley's objectivity. It is difficult to understand how Wesley could justify his ordaining with the statements we just read where he claimed never to have deviated from the doctrines of the Church of England and to always have been faithful to its disciplines.

We gather here and there from his writings that Wesley was never entirely comfortable with what he had done concerning ordination nor with his explanations and justifications. Though one might question Wesley's objectivity over this matter it would be unfair to question his honesty. When at the end of a long life he says that though his approach and emphases may have differed from that of the Church of England, he did not depart from her doctrines, we are safe in believing that he meant what he said and believed it to be entirely true.

This does not mean that others examining Wesley's writings, might not find discrepancy between his theology and that of the Church of England. It is simply to say that Wesley, himself, did not believe that he had written a new theology.

Frederick A Norwood writes in his book, The Story of American Methodism,

> At first sight it would appear that John Wesley had more theological legs to stand on than he

really needed. Various studies of his thought have been made, and it seems that each scholar has found a different leg on which the venerable founder was said to be standing theologically. They are all right inpart.[10]

Norwood points out the magnitude of the problem of tracing Wesley's theological roots, or as he put it, the theological legs on which Wesley stood. This may be a problem for those who study Wesley's theology. It would seem that it was not a problem to Wesley. As has been stated, he saw himself as standing firmly within the Church of England. One could argue that Wesley did some things and said and wrote other things that made his position within the Church of England somewhat precarious. Wesley would have disagreed with that. In 1789, at the age of eighty-six, after sixty years of ministry, he wrote an essay titled, *Further Thoughts on Separation from the Church,* Wesley, of course meant the Church of England. In this essay Wesley claims that his theology had not changed at the end of his ministry from what it had been from his ordination in 1725. He began the essay with these words:

From a child I was taught to love and reverence the Scriptures, the oracles of God; and next to these to esteem the primitive Fathers, the writers of the first three centuries. Next after the primitive church, I esteem our own, the most scriptural, natural church in the world. I therefore not only assent to all her doctrines, but also observe the entire rubric in the Liturgy; with all possible exactness, even at the peril of my life.[11]

As an aside, those who claim that Wesley was a very different person after Aldersgate than before and that after his Aldersgate conversion he gave up his sacerdotalism (reliance on the sacraments and liturgy) are ignoring Wesley's own testimony on the subject.

Howard A. Snyder, in his book, *The Radical Wesley*, wrote:

> It was from his Anglican roots that Wesley drew his catholicity and his high regard for the sacraments. Wesley was not, as the more radical Protestants of his day, staunchly anti-Roman. He was a student of the early Church Fathers and was well versed in the literature of the Roman Catholic mystics. He recognized the debt in devotional literature and liturgical forms owed the Roman Catholic Church. Wesley shared the Anglican view that the Church of England which he always spoke of as the best of all churches, most scriptural of all churches, was the "via media" the middle ground between Catholicism and Protestanism[12]

In his, *A Letter to a Roman Catholic,* Wesley recognized both churches, his and theirs, as parts of the universal Church of Jesus Christ with a shared task of building the Kingdom of God. Though Wesley had serious points of difference with the Roman Catholic Church he recognized the debt owed to it and its place in the Christian Community.

MORAVIAN ROOTS:

Wesley's first exposure to the Moravians was apparently on his crossing from England to Georgia in 1735. On the crossing there occurred a serious storm. Some feared the ship would go down. Apparently Wesley shared this fear along with the fear of dying. He noticed that a religious group of Germans, known as the Moravian Brethren seemed to be totally without fear. He marveled at their faith and envied them their assurance of God's care in life or death. For the rest of the trip he spent time with them in learning German and in religious conversation.

On his return to England, Wesley fell under the influence of another Moravian, Peter Bohler who insisted that faith was all that one needed to receive the assurance that sins past and present were forgiven, and that faith was a gift from God to all who persevered in seeking the gift. That, according to the Moravians, was the sum total of Christianity and it brought peace and tranquility to the human heart. Good works and the sacraments were of little or no value in their view.

Wesley's Aldergate conversion was definitely in the Moravian mold. Wesley, until that time, had seen good works as pretty much all of religion and had earned the name Methodist because of the methodical way in which he and his friends and followers approached good works, including prayer, worship and attendance at the Lord's Supper.

Following his Aldersgate experience in 1738 Wesley went to Germany to visit a religious community under the leadership of Count Ludwig von Zinzendorf. Even after his Aldersgate experience Wesley was plagued with a lack of assurance concerning his salvation. This, according to Zinzendorf was proof that Wesley did not have sufficient faith.

On one occasion, Wesley's friend who had traveled to Germany with him was allowed to partake of Holy Communion with the Moravians while Wesley was not because he was perceived as a troubled person, an indication that he lacked faith and that he relied too much on the means of grace rather than on faith alone. Though Wesley gave no indication of annoyance over this rejection at that time, one can only imagine how the incident affected him. Wesley was later to teach that Holy Communion in itself could be a converting experience.

Though Wesley's heart was "strangely warmed" at Aldersgate, his Moravian friends who had been urging just such an experience on him had their doubts concerning its validity since Wesley did not experience the tranquility and joy their faith gave them. Following his Aldergate experience Wesley continued to be plagued by doubts concerning his relationship to God.

Back in England Wesley remained for a time under the spiritual guidance of Peter Bohler. After

Bohler's return to Germany, Wesley assumed a leadership role among the Moravians in the Fetter Lane society. Wesley however was soon to part ways with the Moravians. The issue that caused Wesley to turn his back on the Moravians was the Moravians total reliance on faith to the total exclusion of works and the Moravians low view of the sacraments. For Wesley to have completely bought into the Moravian approach would have been to sever his relationship with the Church of England, a relationship that was precious to Wesley.

Wesley and several of his followers left the Fetter Lane society and began a new society in the Foundry, a building in which cannon had been manufactured for the British military. The importance of this move in the history of Methodism cannot be overstated. Methodism would develop, under the leadership of Wesley, much different than Moravianism, and would remain, at least while Wesley lived well within The Church of England.

Though Wesley's brush with the Moravians ended when the new society began meeting in the Foundry, some Moravian influence continued in Methodist practice, such as the possibility of entering, by faith, into an instantaneous conversion experience. The preaching of this possibility was a major part of the Wesleyan evangelical revival in England and later in America. Though Methodism was to remain more closely related to Anglicanism, the Moravians definitely left their stamp on Methodism.

The late Albert Outler, one of Methodism's greatest Wesley scholars, in writing of Wesley as a theologian said,

> He was by talent and intent, a folk theologian: an eclectic who had mastered the secret of plastic synthesis, simple profundity, the common touch. He was an effective evangelist guided by a discriminating theological understanding, a creative theologian practically involved in the application of his doctrines in the renewal of the church.

> Few of his doctrinal views are obtuse and none is original. It is their sum and balance that is unique, that gives him a distinctive theological stance. The elements of his theology were adapted form many sources. [13]

Outler then deals with the sources of Wesley's unique theological blend. The answer to the question with which this chapter began must still be, yes; there are some differences between Wesley's theology and that of the Church of England. As Albert Outler wrote:

> Wesley's theology is self –consciously Anglican, but its exact counterpart is not to be found anywhere else in that tradition. There are features in his position derived from left-wing Protestantism – field preaching, lay preaching, "the witness of the Holy Spirit", extempore prayer in the congregation,

etc. – and these greatly alarmed his fellow Anglicans, who saw in them the fatal flaw of 'enthusiasm". Yet his violent aversion to anti-nomianism is clearly catholic – and so are his basic arguments against Calvinistic predestinarianism.[14]

Wesley may have been, as Albert Outler says, self-consciously Anglican, but his eclectic and pragmatic approach to theology may well have taken him further from Anglican than even he realized. It is significant that once his strong guiding hand was removed from the Methodist movement in America by the successful outcome of the American Revolution and in England by Wesley's death, that both the Methodist and Anglicans saw enough differences to prompt separation.

Since that separation those differences have become more clearly defined and more pronounced. In succeeding chapters we will examine the impact of the American Frontier in the nineteenth century on Methodist theology that took it even further from Wesley's theology and practice, a theology Wesley believed to have been purely Anglican.

Throughout his entire life Wesley seems to have been uneasy in his own mind concerning his duty of submission to the authority of the Episcopacy of the Church of England, which he desired to remain firmly within, and his duty to some practices to which he felt God was calling him in order to win souls. He recognized that his ordaining of clergy for America was highly irregular and endangered his relationship with the Church of England. He gave several rationalizations for the move, but never seemed completely comfortable with it. In a letter to a Rev. James Clark, 3 July 1757, he wrote as follows:

> As to my judgment, I still believe "the episcopal form of church government to be scriptural and apostoloical." I mean well agreeing with the practices and writings of the Apostles. But that it is prescribed in Scripture, I do not believe. This opinion which I once zealously espoused, I have been heartily ashamed of since I read Bishop Stillinfleet's "Irenicon". I think he has unanswerably proved that neither Christ or his Apostles prescribed any particular form of church government, and that the plea of divine right for diocesan episcopacy was never heard of in the primitive church. [15]

It becomes obvious as one reads Wesley that he loved the Church of England and sought to be loyal to it, but that he, at times, found himself in some conflict with his beloved church because of his faithfulness to the work that he felt God had called him, the evangelical revival in eighteenth century England.

Wesley seemed almost unaware that different traditions were drawing him in different directions. As we look back on Wesley we can see that the Puritan (dissenting) tradition, the Moravian tradition and the Anglican tradition all played a role in his religious thought and practice. Part of the genius of

Wesley was his ability to incorporate these various theological strains into a coherent whole that met the needs of the evangelical revival that he was so instrumental in starting and maintaining.

Could it be that one of God's callings on John Wesley's life was to be the task of melding the best of several traditions into a practical, scriptural and life changing religion?

CHAPTER THREE:
DISTINCTIVE FEATURES
OF WESLEY'S
THEOLOGY

J ohn Wesley seemed to believe, or perhaps preferred to believe, that there was nothing distinctive about his approach to theology. When pressed on the matter he always maintained that his doctrines were the doctrines of the Church of England. Yet, as was seen in the last chapter, there were many influences other than Anglicanism, impacting Wesley's theological development that molded that theology into something quite different than pure Anglicanism. We will see in the coming chapters that Wesley said, wrote and even did some things that put him outside orthodox Anglicanism. His failure to recognize this is somewhat of a mystery. Throughout his life he spent a great deal of time and ink explaining that what he said and did fit well within the theology of the Church of England. It seems to have been a blind spot with Wesley that what he said and did would eventually and inevitably separate Methodism from the Church of England. Wesley may have used the doctrines of the Church of England but his particular use of them was quite different.

Though the doctrine of Christian perfection was not original with Wesley, he put his own distinctive stamp on that doctrine and made it the centerpiece of Wesleyan theology. No where else, certainly not in Anglicanism, can one find its exact pattern.

As we will see in a later chapter, his understanding of the doctrine of grace, also gave that doctrine a distinctive Wesleyan flavor. Unfortunately, these distinctive Wesleyan doctrines, Christian perfection and grace, suffered some real change on the American frontier.

In the third chapter of his book, *The Bible in the Wesleyan Heritage*, Mack B. Stokes lists the six doctrines he believed Wesley held to be of vital importance. According to Bishop Stokes, Wesley's particular approach to these six doctrines and the balance in which he held them resulted from his total reliance on the Bible as the source of, and test of all doctrines. That is, Wesley measured all doctrine against his understanding of scripture. That is what Wesley meant when he said that he was a man of one book. He certainly did not mean he read only the Bible. He read widely. What he meant was that for him the Bible was the final authority on all matters of doctrine. Nothing that contradicted the Bible could be true. All doctrine must meet that criteria.

The first doctrine in Stokes' list is the **Universality of Sin.** Stokes apparently equated Universal Sin with Original Sin or Birth Sin, as Wesley seemed to do in his sermon, *Original Sin*, and in his longer treatise on the subject titled, *The Doctrine of Original Sin.* In both these works Wesley stressed the universality of sin in humankind, the total corruption of humans and thus their utter dependence on God's Grace. In this matter Wesley seemed to have been in complete accord with orthodox Protestant thought. As we will see later, his suggestion of good works as a prelude to justification, though not a prerequisite for it, opened him up to some criticism; raising questions about his faithfulness to the cardinal Protestant doctrine of salvation by faith alone. Wesley does appear closer to Roman Catholicism on the matter of good works than were most Protestants of his time. This author finds a certain ambiguity in Wesley at this point. Certainly Wesley would not have joined Martin Luther in discarding of the book of James, calling it a "book of straw". Nor would he have written in the margin of his New Testament at Ephesians 2: 8 as Luther did, sola fide, making the passage read, "For by grace you have been saved through faith alone..." Wesley would have been more inclined to agree with James when he said, So faith by itself, if it has no works is dead" (James 2:17).

Wesley seems to have been in full accord with the Ninth Article of Religion of the Church of England, "Of Original Sin or Birth Sin". He passed this article along to American Methodists in a somewhat abridged form as Article VII of the Articles of Religion of the Methodists Episcopal Church in North America. Though abridged, the version given to American Methodists was no less anti-pelagian than the Anglican version. (Pelagius was a fourth century English monk who denied original or birth sin.) Wesley wrote in his sermon, *Original Sin*, of original sin as a disease and of Jesus Christ "as God's method of healing the human soul that is so diseased."[1]

Next in his list of Wesley's most important doctrines Stokes lists **Prevenient Grace,** which in a very real sense is made necessary by the doctrine of original sin. This is especially true for an Arminian which Wesley definitely was.

The doctrine of Prevenient Grace or as Wesley sometimes called it Preventing Grace is the Arminian answer to the Calvinistic Doctrine of election and predestination. Both Arminians and Calvinists agree that it is God's grace that saves humans from the consequences of their sins. The difference between the two is the proportion of divine and human participation in salvation. The question might well be raised here as to just how a totally depraved person, corrupt in heart and mind, a sinner from birth, responds to God's grace. The Calvinists answer would be that only the elect respond because they have been predestined to respond, all others are predestined to be damned. The Arminian response to that is prevenient grace, that grace which taking the initiative, woos every human soul to respond to God's love.

In Wesleyan theology prevenient grace is available to everyone, though some obviously do not respond to it. Wesley, as an Arminian, saw the doctrine of prevenient grace to be of vital importance to human salvation.

The next vital doctrine for Wesley in Stokes list is the most Protestant of all doctrines, **Justification by Faith**. Wesley stood with St. Paul, St. Augustine and Martin Luther on this doctrine. We may safely conclude form Wesley's many statements on the subject that he was in full agreement with Paul, as Paul wrote to the Ephesians, " For by grace you are saved through faith; and this not of your own doing, it is the gift of God, lest any person should boast." (Ephesians 2:8-9) It is a bit difficult to pin Wesley at this point since he advocated for good works both before and after justification. It is obvious that Wesley accepted the cardinal Protestant doctrine of salvation, justification by faith. But he saw good works as the result and sign of salvation. He would have said a hearty amen to James statement, " Faith without works is dead."

For Wesley as for most Christians, justification by faith was made possible by Jesus Christ's death on the cross. This Wesley accepted without reservation or explanation other than it was the teaching of Holy Scripture.

Stokes places the **New Birth** fourth on his list. It should be noted that Wesley did not equate justification with the new birth. New birth is the result of justification. In justification one's sins are no longer counted against one. New birth comes immediately with justification and it is what it means to become a 'new creation in Christ". It may be said that justification is the act and new birth is the result. Wesley describes the new birth in his sermon by that name as follows:

It is that great change which God works in the soul when he brings it into life; when he raises it from a change wrought in the whole soul by the almighty Spirit of God, when it is "created anew in Christ Jesus"; when it is "renewed after the image of God in righteousness and true holiness"; when the love of the world is changed into the love of God; pride into humility, passion into meekness; hatred, envy, malice, into a sincere, tender, disinterested love for all mankind.[2]

Concerning the relationship between justification and the new birth, Wesley wrote in the same sermon, *New Birth,* as follows.

If any doctrines within the whole compass of Christianity may be properly termed fundamental, they are doubtlessly these two, the doctrine of justification and that of the new birth: the former relating to that great work which God does for us, in forgiving our sin; the later, to that great work God does in renewing our fallen natures. In order of time neither of these is before the other; in the moment we are justified by the grace of God, through the redemption that is in Jesus, we are also "born of the Spirit"; but in order of thinking as it is termed, justification precedes the new birth. We first conceive his wrath to be turned away, and then His Spirit to work in our hearts.[3]

The separation of justification and new birth into two simultaneous experiences, closely related, but nevertheless distinct doctrines, and both the works of grace, seems to be unique to Wesley. Perhaps it is a distinction, the importance of which may elude some of us. For Luther and Calvin the distinction did not seem important, though it was recognized. Van A. Harvey wrote in his, *Handbook of Theological Terms*, in presenting their views as follows:

Justification is the act of divine forgiveness whereby, because of the sacrifice of Christ, an unworthy man no longer has his guilt reckoned against him. Accepting that pardon by faith the unworthy man is renewed in his heart.[4]

Wesley is careful to point out in his sermon, *New Birth*, that in the Articles of Religion of the Church of England, that the article on baptism, (No.XXVII) does not equate new birth with baptism. Wesley gave this article, in an abridged form, to the Methodist Episcopal Church of North America as Article XVII.

As we shall see later, new birth is essential to Wesley's signature doctrine, sanctification or Christian Perfection in love, as the first step on the journey. This sanctification according to Wesley had the possibility of being achieved in this life, but was usually achieved at the moment of death, "the moment the soul leaves the body". Wesley was somewhat ambiguous at this point and in later life came to accept the idea that this perfection could be achieved during one's life. We will see in a later chapter how profoundly distorted this signature doctrine of Wesley's theology became on the American frontier in the mid-nineteenth century.

The next important vital doctrine in Stoke's list is **The Witness of the Spirit.** Concerning the witness of the Spirit Wesley wrote, in a sermon by that name:

> By the testimony of the spirit, I mean an inward impression on the soul, whereby the Spirit of God immediately and directly witnesses to my spirit, that I am a child of God; that Jesus Christ has loved me, and given himself for me; that all my sins are blotted out, and I, even I am reconciled to God.[6]

That same paragraph appears in his second sermon on the *Witness of the Spirit*. The witness of the Spirit apparently follows after justification and new birth, but unlike the two former is not necessary to salvation. It is a bonus gift from a loving God.

One of the things this author would like to ask Wesley, if he should ever gain an audience with him on the other side, is to differentiate between what he said about the new birth and what he said about the witness of the Spirit. He finished the paragraph on the new birth, which we examined a few pages back, with these words, "We first conceive his wrath to be turned away, and then the Spirit to work in our hearts." This sounds very much like what he wrote in all three of his sermons on the witness of the Spirit..."By the testimony of the Spirit, I mean an inward impression...that all my sins are blotted out, and I, even I am reconciled to God." Obviously it is this author who lacks understanding.

For Wesley the witness of the Spirit was important because of the very real danger of presuming that one was a child of God when one was not. In his first sermon titled, *The Witness of the Spirit*, Wesley warns against that presumptuousness and lists five marks, which he found in the Bible, for determining if one were truly a child of God.

1. Conviction of sin and repentance always precede the witness of the Spirit. God has promised forgiveness to all "whom with hearty repentance and true faith turn to him."
2. transformed lives, "a vast and mighty change,"
3. Joy in the Lord.
4. The inner witness is present when we love to obey God.
5. A good conscience toward God.

These five marks, according to Wesley, were all present in the life of one who had the witness of the Spirit that he was a child of God. That life was also marked by peace, humility, patience, long - suffering, and gentleness.

In Stoke's list of Wesley's six most important vital doctrines the last one is **Sanctification.** Wesley's teaching on this doctrine and his special emphasis, borrowing as he did from many sources, is arguably the most distinctive feature of his theology. It is with this doctrine that this author finds the greatest deviation form Wesley's teachings, by American Methodists in the nineteenth century.

An important aspect of Wesley's theology is that it was absolutely biblical, the scriptures being the final authority on all matters of doctrine. This is certainly a very Protestant approach to theology. The Protestant problem, however, was not everyone interpreted the scripture in the same way, thus the proliferation of Protestant sects. What may have been distinctive to Wesley was his use of what Albert Outler coined "The Wesleyan Quadrilateral" which made all doctrine subject not only to scripture, but also to the tests of experience, reason, and tradition. Of these four, scripture was always first. There has been some debate about the order in importance of the rest. The most commonly agreed upon order can be demonstrated with the acronym, SERT, with scripture first, then experience, reason, and tradition in that descending order. Wesley would have denied that experience was equal to scripture and saw that as the error of enthusiasts (Quakers and mystics). He

JOHN WESLEY and the AMERICAN FRONTIER

would have denied that reason was equal to scripture and saw that as the error of the deists. Wesley would have denied that tradition was equal to scripture and saw that as the error of the Roman Catholics.

Wesley spoke often of himself "as a man of one book". By this he did not mean that he read only the Bible and that he did not read widely in other disciplines. Wesley was very much a scholar and read widely in many areas. What he did mean by being "a man of one book" was that for him the Bible was the final authority, the final test against which all else was measured. Albert Outler said of Wesley's theology:

Few of his doctrines are obtuse and none is original. It is the sum and balance that is unique, that gives him a distinctive theological stance. The elements of his theology were adapted from many sources: the prime article of justification by faith, from the reformers (Anglican) of the sixteenth century; the emphasis on assurance of faith from the Moravian pietists; the ethical notion of divine and human synergism, from the ancient Fathers of the Church; the idea of the Christian life as devotion, from Taylor, a Kempis, Law (and Scougal), the vision and program of "perfection" from Gregory of Nyssa via "Marcarius". These diverse motifs - mildly incongruous in the theological climate of the early eighteenth century - bought and held together within the frame of the Book of Common Prayer, the Articles and Homilies. But their development in his mind was ordered by the practical exigencies of the Revival itself. Wesley's theology was self-consciously Anglican, but its exact counter-

61

part is not to be found anywhere else in that tradition. There are features from left wing Protestantism - field preaching, lay preaching, "the witness of the Spirit", extempore prayer in the congregation, etc. and these greatly alarmed his fellow Anglicans who saw in them the fatal flaw of "enthusiasm". Yet his violent aversion to antinomianism is clearly catholic - and so are his basic arguments against Calvinistic predestination.[5]

The above quote from Outler supports the conclusion that this author has come to; namely that Wesley's doctrines, or his use of them, were not original with him, but borrowed from many sources. Wesley's originality and what made his theology unique was the use he made of these doctrines, the particular emphasis and balance he gave them which became the norm for early Wesleyan theology.

We will see in later chapters that Wesley's unique approach to certain doctrines, drawing as he did from many sources, and weaving them together into a coherent whole, gave his doctrines of grace and Christian perfection distinctive appearances. In Wesley's theology, neither of these doctrines could be understood without the other. These two doctrines as taught by Wesley, became the signature doctrines of Wesleyan theology. It was to be these two doctrines that suffered most on the American frontier in the nineteenth century.

Thanks to the scholarship of Bishop Mack B. Stokes and that of Dr. Albert Outler, we have in this chapter received a concise introduction to the theology of John Wesley.

CHAPTER FOUR: THE DOCTRINE OF GRACE IN WESLEY'S THEOLOGY

Wesley's unique approach to the Doctrine of Grace was the foundation upon which his whole theology rested and the motivating force for his life's work. The proclaiming of God's grace to a sinful human race was what the Wesleyan revival in the British Isles was all about. American Methodism during the westward expansion was faithful to Wesley at this point. The frontier preacher's motivation was to make God's grace known to sinners and by so doing save them from the "wrath to come".

Grace is the essential ingredient in all Christian theology: Roman Catholic, Orthodox, Protestant (Calvinistic or Arminian). In arriving at his doctrine of grace Wesley drew from a number of sources and using his own experiential and pragmatic approach fashioned a doctrine of grace uniquely Wesleyan.

There is an inherent tension between the concept of God's absolute sovereignty in the matter of salvation and the concept of human free will which allows humans to accept or reject God's offered salvation. Scripture passages from the New Testament can be cited to support each of these diametrically opposing views. Proof testing has been an ongoing game for centuries and has done little or nothing to shed light on the matter. Most of the passages sited are inconclusive. As a generality, there does seem to be a difference in Jesus' emphasis and Paul's, Jesus being more inclusive.

It becomes pretty much a matter of preference; does one prefer to believe that God created some people to be saved and all others to be eternally damned or does one prefer to believe that when Jesus said, " If I be lifted up from the earth I will draw all people to myself" (John 12:32), he included everyone in that, all. John Wesley preferred the latter and did some serious debating through his writings with the opposing view.

Wesley however did not see this theological divide among Christians to be a matter for dividing Christians. For Wesley it was not so much a matter of God's sovereignty versus human free will, but rather a matter of God's free grace. In this approach Wesley created a partial bridge between two opposing views and made it possible for Calvinists and Arminians to work together in the evangelical revival.

What exactly did Wesley mean by grace? In her book, *Wesleyan – Arminian Theology,* Mildred Bangs

Wynkoop gives the following definition of Wesley's doctrine of grace:

> Wesley believed the Bible taught another meaning of Grace stemming out of another concept of God. In some contrast to Calvinism which emphasized the majestic power of God (He creates and redeems because he can do so) and Arminians who emphasized the justice of God. (He is not only good but fair to all men), Wesley emphasized the love of God which takes up and unifies all the attributes of God's total personality. God's acts do not arise out of his creative will or out of a necessity of any kind, but out of his love. God's grace is God's love in action. Grace is the expression of God's moral freedom.[1]

An understanding of that definition of Grace is essential to understanding John Wesley's theology. As Wynkoop points out, Wesley did not preach "free will" in opposition to Calvinism, rather he preached "free grace" in God. Wynkoop expanded her definition of Wesley's doctrine of grace with these words:

> Grace is the majestic expression of God's great love. Creation is the revelation of God's great love; hence it is grace. Grace accounts for all that man is. Man, even fresh from God's hand has no natural ability apart from the immediate application of God's grace. It was "free grace" "That formed man out of the

dust of the ground' and made him in God's image, and gave him the power of dominion. The same "free grace" continues to sustain us in life and whatever human powers and goodness may yet be ours.[2]

In Wesley's theology God's grace, as expressed to the human race, is Christocentric. It is the outpouring of God's love through Jesus Christ. Since grace is the outpouring of God's personality, which is love, there are not different kinds of grace accomplishing different results in humans. There is only one grace, God's love. It is still helpful to speak about grace in terms of its various functions, such as prevenient grace, saving grace, sanctifying grace, etc. but we must always keep in mind that in Wesley's theology there is only one grace, the expression of God's love through Jesus Christ. John did not write in his first Epistle, God loves. He wrote God is love. (I john 4:7)

In Wesley's theology the different ways in which we speak of grace are the different ways in which we humans appropriate God's grace, i.e. God's love in our lives. A distinction must be kept in mind here, if we are to have a clear understanding of Wesley's theology, grace is not something we receive, for it is not a thing at all. It is God himself, a living person-ality, becoming available to our personalities, estab-lishing a relationship with us.

Wesley's unique emphasis on grace as it relates to human salvation can best be seen in his sermons on the theme.

One of the major points at which Wesley was in opposition to Calvinism was at the point of the Calvinistic teaching of "irresistible grace" which meant that if you were predestined to be saved you could not refuse to accept salvation. For Wesley it was not a matter of God's will being imposed on one to effect one's salvation, rather it was a matter of God's love drawing one to respond to God's love with love.

Though passages can be found in Wesley's works which would seem to indicate the contrary, it seems that Wesley did not accept the 'total depravity" of human nature. The fall may have badly marred the image of God in humanity, but it did not completely extinguish it because to have completely destroyed the image of God in humanity would be to rob humanity of that which makes it human, namely, being in the image of God. Wesley is very clear that any vestige of the image of God in fallen human nature is the result of the free grace of God. Without God's grace there would be no image of God in fallen human nature. The grace of God is present in and to all humans to be appropriated for their salvation if they should so choose.

Wynkoop writes in pointing out the difference between Wesley's thought and Calvinism at the point of when and how grace first touches a person's fallen nature:

In Calvinism, man's free will is moved by grace prior to man's consciousness of it and apart from his awareness of it. Regeneration precedes all faith and obedience and is applied to the elect only. In Wesleyanism, "grace, or the love of God, whence cometh our salvation, is free in all, and free for all."[3]

In this passage Wynkoop is quoting from Wesley's sermon, *Free Grace*,

In his sermon, *Original Sin*, based on Genesis 6:5, Wesley contrasted the optimistic view of human nature which stemmed from the humanism so prevalent in eighteenth century England, and which was permeating the church, with the teachings of the Bible as he understood them. Concerning people before the flood he writes:

However, it was still a matter of inquiry 'Was there no remission of evil? Were there no lucid intervals, wherein something good might be found in the heart of man? We are not to consider here, what the grace of God might occasionally work in his soul; and abstracted from this, we have no reason to believe, there was any intermission of that evil. For God, who 'saw the whole imagination of the thoughts of his heart to be evil,' saw likewise, that it was always the same, that 'was only evil continually;' every year, every day, every hour, every moment.' He never deviated toward God.[4]

Wesley continuing in that sermon, *Original Sin*, found human nature to be in the same deplorable state following the flood as it had been before the flood.

When Wesley's sermon *Original Sin* is placed side by side to his sermon, *Working Out Our Own Salvation*, they seem to demonstrate an inconsistency in Wesley's thought. The former emphasizes one's utter inability to act on behalf of one's own salvation. The latter urges people to do good works as a step towards salvation. Wesley even advocated receiving Holy Communion prior to justification as a step toward salvation. In his sermon, *Working Out Our Own Salvation*, Wesley writes these words:

If ever you should desire that God work in you that faith whereby cometh both present and eternal salvation, by the grace already given fly from all sin as from the face of a serpent; carefully avoid every evil work; yea, even abstain from all appearance of evil. And 'learn to do well: Be zealous of good works, works of piety, as well as works of mercy: family prayers and crying to God in secret...

At every opportunity be a partaker of the Lord's Supper...

Deny your self every pleasure which does not prepare you for taking pleasure in God, and willingly embrace every means of drawing near to God, though it be a cross, though it be grievous to the flesh and blood. Thus when you have redemption in the blood of Christ, you will 'go in the light', till walking in the light, 'you are enabled to testify, that He is faithful and just not only to forgive your sins, but to cleanse from all unrightousness,'[5]

Wesley was called by some a papist because of his insistence on good works, even as a necessary step toward salvation. On the other hand Wesley was at times accused of relying on faith alone to the exclusion of works. This "quietism or stillness" was a direct result of the Moravian influence on him.

Wesley's insistence, right after his Aldersgate heart warming experience, that until the moment of that experience he had not been a Christian at all, caused great consternation among his friends and opened him up to criticism that he had become an "enthusiast" and turned his back on the teachings of his church. Wesley later said he had overemphasized the Aldersgate experience in his life.

The apparent inconsistency at this point came from Wesley being Wesley. He could never stop speaking and writing in an authoritative manner from what ever theological position he held at any given moment. When one places his testimony following Aldersgate side by side with his sermon, *Working Out Our Own Salvation*, there is definitely a difference in understanding. In his enthusiasm Wesley was at time given to over stating a position. As was stated early in this book, when the question is raised as to what Wesley taught about a certain subject, one must always ask, when? Wesley freely admitted several times during his life that he had changed his mind. What Wesley came up with as his mature teaching concerning the place of faith and works in salvation was a balance that was both scriptural and practical. Balance is a big word in Wesley's theology and his mature thought on different aspects of theology was invariably a workable balance, scriptural and practical.

If Wesley had waited to write and teach until he had arrived at his mature theological balances his theology would probably have been free from the criticism of inconsistency, and there would probably not have been a great evangelical revival in the English speaking world. His over ruling passion as an evangelist was to bring people into a vital relationship with God through Jesus Christ as Lord and Savior. In his eagerness to do that he shared wholeheartedly with others where he himself was at that moment in his spiritual journey.

If we were to lose sight of Wesley's unique definition of grace and its application to the human condition these apparent inconsistencies in his thought would be irreconcilable. The following passage from the sermon, *Working Out Our Own Salvation*, demonstrates the manner in which his definition of grace spares Wesley from the charge of inconsistency.

> For allowing that all souls of men are dead in sin by nature, this excuses none, seeing that no man is in state of mere nature; there is no man, unless he has quenched the Spirit that is wholly void of the grace of God.

No man living is entirely destitute of what is vulgarly called natural conscience. But this is not natural: It is more properly termed, preventing grace....

So that no man sins because he does not have grace, but because he does not use the grace which he hath. [6]

As we have seen preventing grace (prevenient grace) is God's love extended to every human, even while in a depraved condition, which draws humans toward God, that spark of the divine, the image of God, in the human soul which makes it human. Or as St. Augustine is so often quoted, "Our souls are restless, O God, until they find their rest in Thee."

For Wesley, then, the various ways in which humans experience grace (God's love) in their lives are prevenient grace (preventing grace); convincing grace; saving grace; and sanctifying grace. Faith for Wesley was trusting in grace (God's love) for all stages of the spiritual journey. The last appropriation of grace is sanctifying grace that results in being saved from the "power and root of sin", and being restored to the image of God. [7]

In summing up, there are two crucial points to remember about Wesley's doctrine of grace. First, grace is God's love in action to draw all human hearts to God's self in a loving relationship. Second, God's love (grace) is available to all humanity, those who accept it and those who reject it. God is love, it is God's nature. It is all inclusive. God cannot stop loving because love is what God is according to St.

John. Wesley's doctrine of grace is simple; and it is scriptural; and it is beautiful; and it is much needed in the world in which we live!

Wesley's Doctrine Of Grace On The American Frontier

It may well have been Wesley's unique approach to the Doctrine of Grace that made Methodism so compatible with the American mindset. As we have seen, Wesley's Doctrine of Grace, by emphasizing God's free grace, God's love for humanity, made room for some human response, if not for some human initiative in salvation. Remember, Wesley advocated good works and pious living, even to the taking of Holy Communion while one was waiting for faith to appropriate God's love in justification.

The emphasis on human freedom and human responsibility in responding to God's grace was well received in a society in which there was a growing emphasis on individuals' freedom, and human initiative.. In short, Wesley's Doctrine of Grace was more compatible with the frontier mindset than was Calvinism with its emphasis on God's arbitrary imposing of God's will in human salvation.

In colonial New England, Calvinism was defined by scholars such as Jonathan Edwards (1703-1758) and his able student Samuel Hopkins (1721-1803). As the colonial period ended and people began moving westward both Calvinism and Wesleyan Theology began to change. Theology was no longer in the hands of scholars and that was to matter greatly.

The titles of two books by two early American Methodists indicates the intensity with which Wesleyan theology engaged Calvinism. The Rev. Wilbur Fisk, D.D., a Methodist, had a book published in 1837 with the engaging title, *Calvinistic Controversy Embracing a Sermon on Predestination and Several Numbers on the Same Subject.* Asa Shinn, a self educated theologian, another Methodist, who if not the best, was the best known defender of Wesleyan theology in his day, had a book published with the title, *An Essay on the Plan of Salvation in Which Several Kinds of Evidence are Examined and Applied to the Government and Moral Attributes of the Deity.* It is obvious from the titles of those two books by early American Wesleyan theologians that American Methodist theology was fashioned in controversy with Calvinism.

As the frontier moved west it seems that Wesley's middle ground of God's free grace was lost sight of and the controversy returned to its original form, human free will versus God's absolute sovereignty. Wesley had directed the controversy away from either extreme. This fine point was lost in the hands of uneducated clergy on both sides of the divide.

As has been stated earlier in this chapter, in Wesley's theology, grace is God's personality, God's nature in action and is available to all people at all times. It only remains for people to respond to that love; the human personality interacting with the divine personality in a vital loving relationship.

This view of grace is supported by Jesus' beautiful story of the Prodigal Son, which is pretty much an illustration and summation of the Gospel. The son who was an out and out sinner, "riotous living" about says it, came to his senses and returned to his father's home. The prodigal had to be made aware of the father's great love for him. But the good son had the same problem, he too was unaware of how much the father loved him, and had to be made aware of the Father's love. (Luke 15:15-32) The father's love was available, always, for the good and the bad. They just had to become aware of it. It would seem like a short jump to universalism. For Wesley there was no such possibility, one still had to accept or reject the offered love.

Since theology in England and Colonial America had been in the hands of scholars, both Calvinists and Arminians could share a common goal of bringing salvation to the masses on both sides of the Atlantic.

George Whitfield, a staunch Calvinist and close friend of Wesley's, since their days at Oxford, worked with him in the revival in England. Whitfield crossed the Atlantic several times on preaching missions and helped to fan the dying embers of the Great Awakening in New England and to spread the revival down the eastern seaboard. The friendship of Wesley and Whitfield waned for a time but as they grew older it was rekindled and Wesley preached Whitfield's funeral sermon.

Following the American Revolution, under the dynamic leadership of Francis Asbury, the Methodist Episcopal Church was organized. The church imme- diately began its westward expansion, moving with the pioneers to, and then beyond the Allegheny

Mountains. The use of circuit riders, an unsettled clergy on horseback, assured that Methodism would always be on the far edge of the frontier, preaching the saving grace of God.

In England Wesley made use of lay-preachers, but he demanded that they be constant students. He prescribed a course of study for them which included the Christian classics, the early church fathers, and even Greek. One wonders if perhaps at the end of Wesley's prescribed course of study these students might not have been more educated for ministry than many modern seminary graduates. Though they were not university trained, it could never be said of them that they were uneducated.

Once Methodism left the Atlantic seaboard and moved west the influence of scholars began to wane and became almost non-existent. As the Methodist Episcopal Church made its rapid numerical growth and the frontier expanded to greater distances there was a great lack of educated men to fill the ranks of the clergy. Circuit riders recruited by other circuit riders and ordained by Bishop Asbury and other bishops who came after him, were often recent converts to Christianity with "warm hearts" and almost no education. There are recorded cases of men learning to read after having been recruited for the ministry. In a latter chapter we will examine the impact made on Methodism be these uneducated clergy. In fairness it must be said that some of these men became self educated to the extent that they spoke and wrote well, and some even made contributions to theological thought. The Rev. Asa Shinn, mentioned earlier, is an excellent example of the self educated men who made real contributions to Methodist theology.

All Protestant denominations, to some extent, and at different time moved westward with the people. Second to the Methodists on the frontier were the Baptists who kept up with the people, as they moved westward, with the use of settled clergy. The farmer/ preacher, who preached on Sunday, baptized, married and buried, and worked his own farm the rest of the time was a common part of many early settlements as they grew into established communities.

It has been said in humor that,"The Methodists went west with the pioneers; the Presbyterians waited for the stagecoach; and the Episcopalians waited for the Pullman car." As with all humor, there is an element of truth in it, but it is unfair to the Baptists who were close to Methodists in reaching the frontier and the Presbyterians and Episcopalians who were to a lesser extent represented on the frontier. It should be noted that the Presbyterians and the Episcopalians required educated clergy.

As with the Methodist approach, so the Baptist approach provided ready supply of dedicated, though uneducated clergy with a great desire to win souls for Christ, and their membership rolls. As the Methodists became less and less under the influence of eastern scholarship so did their Baptist counterparts. As has been pointed out, in that climate the battle lines were more clearly drawn between Calvinism's predesti-nation and Arminianism's free will. An uneducated frontier Methodist clergy pretty much lost sight of Wesley's middle ground between predestination and free grace, Wesley's understanding of God's free grace may not have completely reconciled Calvinism and Arminianism, but it knocked off some of the rough edges of the controversy and allowed them to share common goals and to work together. Unfortunately this middle ground was lost on the frontier. This author believes that this loss was largely because of an uneducated clergy in both camps and their simplistic approaches.

In 1821, the flamboyant Methodist circuit rider, Peter Cartwright, who left an account of his labors in his autobiography, wrote of a visit he had in the home of a family he derogatorily spoke of as 'high toned predestination Baptists". He tells of a camp meeting he conducted in the vicinity the following year, in which part of the family was "powerfull converted and joined the Methodist Church". This quote points out the strength of the conflict over the doctrine of grace. In Cartwright's view the Baptist family needed to be "powerfull converted" before they could see the light of free will, and the Methodist way.

In this chapter we have placed the loss of a unique aspect of Wesley's doctrine of grace, with its emphasis on free grace, on an uneducated clergy. An uneducated clergy was probably the biggest factor in the Americanization of Wesley's doctrine of grace. In chapter one it was posited, however, that there were four factors of frontier life that impacted on John Wesley's theology to Americanize it, 1. uneducated clergy, 2. plurality of religious groups, 3.the American mindset, 4. camp meeting/revivalism. It can readily be seen that all four factors were to some extent at play in molding the American version of Wesley's doctrine of grace.

CHAPTER FIVE: WESLEY'S DOCTRINE OF CHRISTIAN PERFECTION

N o other doctrine has come to distinguish Wesleyan theology from other Protestant theologies to so great an extent as has Wesley's unique approach to the doctrine of Christian perfection, or holiness, or sanctification, or perfect love, or perfect intentions, all terms used interchangeably by Wesley in his preaching and writing. His particular approach to Christian perfection is not found anywhere else in Anglicanism. And yet, as with his approach to all matters of theology, Wesley did not see himself as an innovator; he saw himself to be well within the mainstream of Anglican theology. Others may have seen him somewhat differently, but Wesley always preferred to see himself within the theological perimeters of his beloved Church of England. In his *Plain Account of Christian Perfection*, Wesley had this to say concerning a conversation he had with Bishop Gibson:

> "I think it was in the latter end of the year 1740, that I had a conversation with Dr. Gibson, then Bishop of London, at Whitehall. He asked me what I meant by perfection. I told him without disguise or reserve. When I had finished speaking, he said, 'Mr. Wesley, if that is what you mean publish it to the world.' 'I answered, my Lord, I will.' and accordingly wrote and published the sermon, on Christian perfection."[1]

It is evident to anyone who has come to know John Wesley through his writings, that Bishop Gibson's approval of his doctrine of Christian perfection was very important to him in that it reinforced for him what he always preferred to believe, that he was preaching and teaching the doctrines of the Church of England and nothing else.

As no other doctrine came to distinguish Wesleyan theology from the other protestant theology to the extent that Wesley's teachings on Christian perfection did, so no other Wesleyan doctrine has been so misunderstood and misconstrued. At least part of the confusion around the doctrine must be laid at Wesley's own doorstep. Wesley's doctrine of Christian perfection was many years in coming to its final form, and through the years he was often ambiguous in explaining it.

When Wesley answered, as he usually did when pressed on the matter, of what he meant by Christian perfection, by quoting Jesus, "You shall love the Lord, your God with all your heart and with all your soul and with all your strength, and your neighbor as yourself." (Luke 10:27) there were few who could disagree with him. As Bishop Gibson told him, "If that's what you mean, publish it to the world."

When the discussions began to swirl around whether one could be made perfect in this life, and if so, when, or whether one could come into the condition instantaneously, or whether one should testify to perfection if one believed one had achieved it, the waters became murky.

When Wesley came to the conclusion that one could be made perfect in love in this life, and began to teach that possibility, his good friend George Whitefield and even his brother, Charles asked, "Where are the perfect ones?" That is a legitimate question. Most of us would settle for one example!

Wesley spent a lot of space in his pamphlet, *A Plain Account of Christian Perfection*, and in his several sermons on Christian perfection, as well as else where, explaining what he did and did not mean by Christian perfection. In sermon numbered XL, *Christian Perfection*, he began with the statement, "I shall endeavor to show first, in what sense Christians are not perfect." In the list of "are nots" he stated that Christians are not free from ignorance; not free from mistakes; not free from infirmities (physical and moral); and not free from temptation. He listed possible infirmities as follows; slowness of understanding, dullness or confusion of apprehension, incoherency of thought, irregular quickness or heaviness of imagination. A little further into the sermon Wesley made this statement:

> "Christian perfection, therefore, does not imply (as some men seem to have imagined) an exemption either from ignorance, or mistake, or infirmity, or temptation. Indeed it is only another term for holiness. They are two names of the same thing. Thus everyone who is holy is in the scriptural sense, perfect. Yet, we may lastly observe that neither in this respect is there any absolute perfection on earth."[3]

The last sentence in that quote raises an interesting question that will be dealt with more fully later in this book, "How many degrees of perfection are there; is there no absolute perfection?" Wesley seems to hold out for several degrees of perfection, babes in Christ, strong young men and fathers in the faith. Wesley stated that even babes in Christ are perfect in a sense. Here Wesley is following John (I John 2:12-14). This scripture indicates that growth and maturing are to be expected at all stages of the Christian's spiritual journey. Wesley, following John, speaking to the fathers said, "I write unto you fathers because you have known both the Father, and the Son, and the Spirit of Christ, in your inner most soul. Ye are 'perfect men' being grown up to the measure of the stature of the fullness of Christ"[4]. Wesley, here, as elsewhere, makes spiritual growth and maturing in the faith, essential elements in Christian perfection. This process, according to Wesley, is to go on from justification and new birth until death. The goal is to grow ever more Christ like, to have "the mind of Christ", to be governed by the inclusive love of Christ.

Few Christians would have trouble with this concept of Christian perfection, the goal being to love God and neighbor and to grow more Christ like as one travels through life. If the doctrine could have been left at that, there would have been much less disagreement about it. There is, of course, a difference between accepting a concept and living it!

The major purpose of the Wesley hymns was to teach doctrine to those who sang them. One of Charles Wesley's hymns, that most clearly states what Christian perfection is, and what it can do for a Christian, is the beloved, *Love Divine, All Loves Excelling*. The second stanza and the fourth are particularly pertinent.

Breath, O breathe thy loving Spirit into every troubled breast! Let us all in thee inherit; let us find that second rest. Take away our bent to sinning; Alpha and Omega be, end of faith as its beginning, set our hearts at liberty.

Finish then thy new creation; pure and spotless let us see thy great salvation perfectly restored in thee; changed from glory into glory, till in heaven we take our place, till we cast our crowns before thee, lost in wonder, love and praise.[5]

In this hymn, Christian perfection is defined as the removal of our bent to sinning, and being filled with Christ's loving spirit. This hymn may well give us a better understanding of Wesley's doctrine of Christian perfection than the sermons and pamphlets'.

As with the development all doctrines, Wesley was catholic and eclectic in his approach to Christian perfection. He was familiar with both the Protestant and Roman Catholic mystics, with the early church fathers, both eastern and western and with German pietism. From all these he borrowed some things and rejected others. Wesley did not invent the term, *Christian Perfection*. William Law wrote a book titled, Christian Perfection, with which Wesley was familiar.. The concept of Christian perfection has had many interpretations through out the history of the church. Some examples of the attempts at Christian perfection are the monastic movement, the early church hermits who withdrew to a solitary life in desert areas, and some mystics who found conversation with God sufficient and avoided all conversation with their fellow humans. The goal for all these was to seek Christian perfection by avoiding polluting contact with the human race. True, many temptations were avoided in this way, but certainly not all.

Wesley was too much of an activist, concerned as much with redemption of society as of the individual, to be caught up in mysticism or pietism (or quietism) as he sometimes called it.

This was one of the issues over which he broke with Moravians. (The other issue was the low regard in which the Moravians held the sacraments and other means of grace.)

For Wesley any religion had to have the practical aspect of changing society for the better, as well as changing the individual. Writing on this matter in his fourth discourse on the Sermon on the Mount, Wesley wrote:

> Many eminent men have spoken this: have advised us to cease from all outward action; wholly to withdraw from the world; to leave the body behind us; to have no concern at all for outward religion, but to work all virtues in the will; as the more excellent way, more perfective of the soul, as well as more acceptable to God. It needed not that any should tell our Lord of this masterpiece of the wisdom from beneath, this fairest of all devises where-with Satan hath ever perverted the right ways of the Lord![6]

A little further along in the discourse, Wesley makes it quite clear that Christianity forces one into a right relationship with other people as well with God.

> First, I shall endeavor to show that Christianity is essentially a social religion; and that to turn it into a solitary religion is to destroy it.

By Christianity I mean that method of worshiping God which is here revealed to man by Jesus Christ. When I say, this is essentially a social religion, I mean not only it cannot subsist so well, but that it cannot subsist at all without society, - with out living and conversing with other men. And in showing this, I shall confine myself to those considerations which will arise from the very discourse before us. But if this be shown, then, doubtless, to turn this religion into a solitary one is to destroy it..[7]

These quotes from Wesley's works and many more that could be cited, clearly demonstrate why Wesley could not be a mystic, or a pietist in the Moravian mold of withdrawal from the world into a contemplative community. For Wesley, the purpose of the experience of Christian perfection was to usher in the kingdom of God, in the midst of humanity. This was to be accomplished as Christians, filled with the love of God and love for their neighbors tackled the ills of society. For Wesley the doctrine of Christian perfection had a very practical application. Its purpose was not to make one feel good, nor to give one spiritual superiority; its purpose was to redeem the world through redeemed people, governed by love. Wesley did not allow for a separation in the Christian religion between personal sanctification and the sanctification of society; they were part and parcel of the same gospel. Wesley's followers on either side of that artificial divide, often seen in the church today, would do well to remember that for Wesley there was no possibility of that divide with out destroying Christianity.

Those who place an undue emphasis on Wesley's Aldersgate experience to the point of not seeing him as really a Christian before that "conversion" experience will find themselves flying in the face of Wesley's latter testimony on the matter. In his *A Plain Account of Christian Perfection*, he writes at length about a sermon he preached on 1 January 1733, five years before Aldersgate, in St. Mary's Church, Oxford University, titled, *The Circumcision of the Heart*, which was, apparently, his first published work. Wesley could write of that sermon in 1777, forty-four years after he first preached it:

> This was the view of religion I had then, which even then I scrupled not to term perfection. This is the view I have of it now, without any material addition or diminution. And what is there here, which any man of understanding, who believes the Bibles, can object to? [8]

In his *A Plain Account of Christian Perfection*, Wesley gave, by way of introduction, four sources for his views on Christian perfection that molded his thinking on the matter, and which became the basis for that early sermon, *Circumcision of the Heart*. He states that in 1725 he first read Bishop Taylor's, *Rule for Holy Living and Dying*. He then wrote:

In reading several parts of the book, I was exceedingly affected; that part in particular which relates to purity of intentions. Instantly I resolved to dedicate all my life to God, all my thoughts, and words, and actions; being thoroughly convinced, there was no medium; but that every part of my life (not only some) must either be sacrifices to God, or to myself, that is in affect to the Devil.[9]

In the year 1726 he read Thomas a' Kempis *Christian Pattern*. This further inclined him to live a life completely devoted to God. He wrote following his introduction to Kempis,

I saw that "simplicity of intentions" and "purity of affection", in all we speak or do, and one desire ruling our tempers, are indeed the "wings of the soul", without which she can never ascend to the mount of God.

A year or two later Wesley read William Law's *Christian Perfection* and also his *A Serious Call to a Devout and Holy Life*, after which he wrote.

These convinced me more than ever of the absolute impossibility of being half a Christian; and I determined through His grace, (the absolute necessity of which I was deeply sensitive of), to give Him my soul, my body, and my substance.[11]

To maintain that the man who wrote these statements concerning Christian Perfection was not yet a Christian and would not be until after his Aldersgate experience is absurd. As we have seen Wesley, himself, claims never to have deviated from that 1733 sermon, *Circumcision of the Heart.* Though Wesley at first said that he had not been a Christian before Aldersgate he later said that he had placed too much emphasis on that experience. Wesley did write and say things that indicated he felt his Aldersgate experience began a new and more productive phase of his Christian life.

An argument can be made, as some have, that his Aldersgate experience was his experience of sanctification or Christian perfection. This is not a strong argument considering Wesley's own testimony. After Aldersgate he seems to have gone from an "I resolve" approach to an "I accept" approach. But to contend that he became a Christian at a little after 9:00 p.m. on 24 May 1738 is to contradict Wesley himself in his later evaluations of the experience.

Albert C. Outler, in his book *Theology in the Wesleyan Spirit,* writes, "Too little attention has been paid to the implications of the fact that Wesley never discarded this sermon (Circumcision of the Heart - 1733) or even recast it." [11] The change that Outler sees as having occurred in Wesley's thinking is in the order of Holiness or "pure intentions" Outler writes of that change:

It is true that in those years, 1725-1738, he consistently misplaced 'holiness' (or pure

intentions) before justification, as prepara-
tory to it. One of his decisive shifts in his
1738 transformation was the reversal of that
order. Thereafter, justification always stands
first, without any antecedent precondition to
human salvation.[12]

In Wesley's thought, only after justification,
can the process of sanctification properly begin as a
maturing process, as one moves toward the goal of
sanctification, Christian maturing, having "the mind
of Christ". Outler then points out what was one of the
major points at which Wesley parted company with
the Moravians and with George Whitfield. Certainly
other issues separated Wesley from Whitefield and
the Moravians (in Whitefield's case, predestination
and what Wesley called quietism in the case of the
Moravians). It is not hard to understand why the
kinetic Wesley, racing around the British Isles, to
save lost souls, would find the sitting and waiting of
the Moravians unacceptable. Outler writes:

This relationship of justification to sanctification
was the critical issue that had first been raised for Wesley
in his encounter with Hernnhuters and Salzburgers in
Georgia. It was the main issue that divided Wesley and
Whitefield almost as soon as the revival began. It was
the issue on which Wesley and Count Zinzendorf soon
clashed and parted company. [13]

All this would indicate, how closely in Wesley's
thinking, justification by grace, through faith, was
tied with sanctification. For Wesley the two could not
be separated. They were part of the same process.

Sanctification began with justification and continued through out the Christian's life as one, through the grace of God, strove to be more perfect in love for God and neighbor, to have the mind of Christ. That love of God translates into love for ones fellow humans. This is expressed in Wesley's oft quoted statement. "Do all the good you can to all the people you can in all the places you can at all times ever you can." For Wesley, the experience of perfect love (sanctification, pure intentions, Christian perfection) was inseparable from social ethics. The purpose of this love was to help usher in that kingdom we so often pray for when we say, "Thy kingdom come, Thy will be done, on earth as it is in heaven." Outler suggests that the coma should come after the earth rather than after done to make sure we understand that His kingdom will not come here on earth until His will is done here on earth, perfectly, as it is presumably done in heaven.

Without careful examination, Wesley's teaching at this point seems to present a contradiction. If faith is the sole requirement for salvation, (and sanctification, which is an integral part of salvation), why should we be busy doing good? Is there not an apparent contradiction here? The Moravians would have answered, yes. Wesley would have answered that question with a resounding, no. Wesley did not see the purpose of sanctification to make one feel good. Its purpose was to make one good, as one grew more Christ like. Being more like Christ meant doing Christ's work, loving and caring for those in need.

In chapter four we saw how closely related in Wesley's thinking were his doctrine of sanctification and his doctrine of grace, prevenient grace, converting grace and sanctifying grace, different functions of the same grace, i.e. God's love.

Early on, Wesley saw Christian perfection as a life long goal, finally arrived at in the instant of death. Latter he came to see it as a possibility in this life. He even came to allow for the possibility of entering into the experience instantaneously as one surrendered one's life completely to God. Wesley, however, never surrendered his belief that Christian perfection was a life long process, as one continued to grow in love for God and others; there was no stopping point before death. This raises another question, "If Christian perfection is a life long process beginning with conversion and new birth, and continuing until death, the instant the soul leaves the body, what is the instantaneous aspect of it, what does it accomplish and why is it needed?" This author cannot find anywhere that Wesley fully cleared up that matter. Again, we might raise the question, "Where are those who have been instantaneously made perfect in love?" This author has known people who professed to have entered instantaneously into that perfect love, and some of them have been very nasty persons. This, of course, is not a valid argument against the teaching, but it does raise some questions.

As we will see in the next chapter, the American Holiness movement taught, and still does, that sanctification is a "second definite work of grace". Wesley saw grace, i.e. God's love, operative at all times in the Christian's life, even before one accepted salvation by faith. Grace acting in its different functions is what holds Wesley's religious thought together.

Wesley's emphasis seems to have been on "going on to perfection", rather than having arrived at it. For his sermon numbered XL, *Christian Perfection*, his text was Philippians 3:12. In this scripture passage, Paul wrote, "Not that I have already obtained this or am already made perfect; but I press on to make it my own. Brethren, I do not consider that I have made it my own; but one thing I do, forgetting what lies behind and straining forward to what lies ahead, I press on toward the goal of the upward call of God in Christ Jesus."

The important thing to remember is that grace acts in the entire process of spiritual growth at all times and the result is that the Christian is able to carry out the two commandments, to love God with all one's heart and one's neighbor as oneself. In his sermon, *On God's Vineyard*, Wesley clearly states the relationship of justification and sanctification:

It is then, a great blessing given to this people, (Methodists) that as they do not think or speak of sanctification so as to supercede justification. They take care to keep each in its own place, laying equal stress on one and the other. They know God has joined these together, and it is not for man to put them asunder. Therefore they maintain, with equal zeal and diligence the doctrine of free, full, present justification, on the one hand and of

entire sanctification both of heart and life
on the other; being as tenacious of outward
(holiness) as any Pharisee. [14]

The last half of that last sentence could cause
some concern with the reference to the holiness of
the Pharisee; we have not been taught to admire the
holiness of the Pharisee! Yet Wesley here, as always,
is insistent on inward holiness being translated into
outward holiness. Wesley could never be accused
of antinomianism. Grace does not free one from the
law!

The criticism of those who say that Wesley taught
salvation by good works is not justified in light of
his teaching on grace. Good works, loving neighbor
as self, is the result of salvation not the cause of
it. Unlike Martin Luther, Wesley would not have
discarded the Epistle of James as, "a book of straw"
because of its emphasis on works. James wrote, "For
just as the body without the spirit is dead, so faith
without works is dead." (James 2:26) Wesley, unlike
Luther, would say a hearty Amen to that statement.

In that same sermon, God's Vineyard, Wesley
asks and answers the question, "Who then is a
Christian?" The answer he gives not only maintains
the relationship between justification and sanctification, but defines sanctification as well.

"Who then is a Christian, according to the
light which God hath vouchsafed to this people?
(Methodists) He that being justified by faith' hath
peace in God through our Lord Jesus Christ, 'born

from above' born of the Spirit'; inwardly changed from the image of the devil, to that 'image of God wherein he was created': he finds the love of God shed abroad in his heart by the Holy Ghost which is given unto him, and whom this love constrains to love his neighbor, every man, as himself; he that has learned from his Lord to be meek and lowly in heart, and in every state to be content; he in whom is that whole mind, all tempers, which are also in Christ Jesus." [15]

Another aspect of Wesley's doctrine of Christian perfection, which is supported by the sermon from which the last two quotes came, is its Christological foundation. The goal for Wesley was to have the "mind of Christ" within one; to become Christ like. Wesley wrote of Martin Luther, that he, Luther, was totally ignorant of the doctrine of sanctification. Yet Luther wrote of striving to be Christ like, saying that we should become "little Christs". Perhaps Wesley was too harsh in his criticism of Luther on this matter and Wesley and Luther were not so far apart as Wesley saw them to be. At any rate, The Christocentric nature of Wesley's doctrine of Christian perfection was well supported in his preaching and writing. We will see in the next chapter that the Christocentric nature of the doctrine suffered on the American frontier.

SOME COMMON QUESTIONS ABOUT THE DOCTRINE AS TAUGHT By WESLEY:

Is sanctification experienced instantaneously as claimed by some, especially in 19th century

America? In Wesley's Journal entry for 29 October 1762, he quotes from a letter he wrote to one of his preachers, Thomas Maxwell, who had been with him from the beginning. This letter takes Maxwell to task for the perversion of Wesley's doctrine of Christian perfection. This letter was written at a time when Wesley's influence was all pervasive and his control almost absolute in the Methodist societies. Yet his doctrine of Christian perfection was already being taken in directions which he found excessive and objectionable. It cannot help but be noted how appropriate these words written in mid-eighteenth century England would have been to Methodists in mid-nineteenth century America. Yet, those words were available.

> I dislike your supposing man....can be absolutely perfect....Your depreciating justification.....appearance of pride......Overvaluing feelings....,.undervaluing reason...littleness Of love..., want of meekness,....bigotry and narrowness of your censoriousness...your offering people sanctification just now,...the bidding them say, 'I believe;...the bitterly condemning any who oppose you...[16]

Thomas Maxwell soon parted company with Wesley and continued to preach his own version of Christian perfection, quite different from Wesley's. The doctrine lost much of its beauty at the hands of some who professed to be Wesley's disciples in both England and America. The letter to Maxwell would seem to indicate that Wesley did not teach instantaneous sanctification, at that time.

Even so astute a Wesley scholar as Albert Outler frankly admits to some confusion about what Wesley did teach concerning an instantaneous experience of sanctification. He does say that according to Wesley's "calendar" the state of sanctification, being perfected in love, was usually entered into at the time of death.[16] By no means would everyone agree with Outler, certainly not the holiness sects that have sprung up out of Methodism and which have made the instantaneous aspect of the experience of prime importance. At the hands of the American Holiness movement, sanctification became an esoteric experience into which the spiritually elite (them) entered into instantly, by faith.

Apparently Wesley did allow later for an instantaneous experience somewhere between justification and death. He insisted, however, on growth and maturing both before and after that experience, this can cause some confusion. It is safe to say that Wesley saw Christian perfection as being perfected in love rather than having been perfected. In the above quoted letter Wesley chided Maxwell for "your offering people sanctification just now".

Did Wesley teach that one should testify to the experience if one felt one had achieved it? Again, his letter to Thomas Maxwell, previously quoted from, partially answers that question. In that letter Wesley chided Maxwell for "bidding them to say, I believe". In a Plain Account of Christian Perfection, Wesley raised the question and answered it.

> Question: Suppose one had attained this, would you advise him, to speak of it?
>
> Answer: At first he would scarce be able to refrain, the fire would be so hot within him; his desire to proclaim the loving - kindness of the Lord carrying him away like a torrent. But afterwards he might; and then it would be advisable, not to speak of it to them that know not God; (it is most likely, it would only provoke them to blaspheme;) nor to others without some particular reason, without some good in view. And then he should have special care to avoid all appearance of boasting; to speak with deepest humility and reverence, giving all glory to God. [17]

Wesley always cautioned against the sin of spiritual pride or presumptuousness.

Does one have the assurance that one has arrived at Christian perfection?

In *Plain Account of Christian Perfection*, Wesley wrote:

> "But I have no witness that I am saved from sin. Yet I have no doubt of it." "Very well: as long as you have no doubt of it, it is enough; when you have need you will have the witness." [18]

This passage seems to tell us that assurance is possible, but also that it is not always necessary. Other passages that could be quoted, are even stronger in asserting that assurance, or witness of the Spirit, can be a part of sanctification or holiness. There are many such passages in Wesley's writings. One such passage, coming from his Sermon No. XI *The Witness of the Spirit*, based on Romans 8:16, states:

But the point is; whether there be any direct testimony of the Spirit at all... I believe there is; because that is the plain, natural meaning of the text, "The Spirit itself beareth witness with our spirit, that we are the children of God." It is manifest here are two witnesses mentioned, who together testify the same thing; the Spirit of God and our own spirit. [19]

The answer to our question concerning the assurance of sanctification is yes, one could have the assurance of the Spirit that one was sanctified. As we have seen, Wesley did allow that one might have to wait for the assurance to be given. For Wesley, one's feeling of assurance or lack thereof was not the criterion of whether one was or was not experiencing Christian perfection. Rather the criterion was the fruits, the results. The real question was, "Is one humble, gentle, patient and loving?"

What was the purpose of sanctification?

For Wesley, the experience of Christian perfection was not meant to be an esoteric experience, to be enjoyed by the few, nor was it meant to be an end in itself. It was to have the very practical aspect of winning others to Christ; and of motivating Christians to social action, the redemption of society; the doing all the good one could, to and for as many as one could; to usher in the Kingdom we so often pray for. This emphasis put British Methodism at the forefront of social struggles such as prison reform, education of the masses, and the fight to abolish slavery. Wesley's oft quoted statement applies here, "The Gospel of Christ knows of no religion but social; no holiness but social holiness. Faith working by love is the length and breadth and height of Christian perfection."

Unlike the American Holiness movement, Wesley did not use Pentecostal language in speaking or writing about Christian perfection. He did not equate Christian perfection with the disciples experience at Pentecost. Wesley saw Christian perfection in Christocentric terms. One was to seek the 'mind of Christ" (a mind governed by love) in order to more perfectly do God's will and work in the world. Wesley invariably equated Christian perfection with fulfilling Jesus' summation of the Law. In *Plain Account of Christian Perfection*, we read:

> Question, 6. What love is this?
> Answer; The loving the Lord our God with all our mind, soul and strength; and loving our neighbor as ourselves, as our own souls. [20]

On 27 January 1767 in London, Wesley wrote a one page essay, titled, *Brief Thoughts on Christian Perfection*. This brief work was apparently to answer some questions that others, and perhaps Wesley, himself, were having concerning Christian perfection. This brief work, with its three points, is worth quoting here because it is a summation of the doctrine approximately thirty years after Aldersgate,

"Some thoughts occurred to my mind this morning concerning Christian perfection, and the manner and time of receiving it, which I believe may be useful to set down.

1. By perfection I mean humble, gentle, patient love of God, and our neighbor, ruling our tempers, words and actions.

    I do not include an impossibility of falling from it, either in part or whole. Therefore I retract several expressions in our hymns, which express, partly imply, such an impossibility.

    And I do not contend for the term sinless, though I do not object to it.

2. As to the manner. I believe that this perfection is wrought in the soul by a simple act of faith; consequently in an instant.

3. As to the time. I believe this instant generally is the instant of death, the moment before the soul leaves the body. But I believe it may be ten, twenty, thirty or forty years before. I believe it usually is many years after justification; but that might be five years or five months after it, I know no conclusive argument to the contrary.

If it must be many years after justification, I would like to know How many.

And how many days or months, or even
years, can anyone allow to be between perfection and death? How far from justification
and how near to death." [21]

In this passage we do not find the assuredness
that we have come to expect from Wesley. Did he
at this late stage really have questions or was this
merely a mode of teaching?

Although Wesley did allow for instantaneous
perfection appropriated by faith, he always seemed
to be a little uneasy about it, as demonstrated in his
letter to Thomas Maxwell sited above. In that letter
he chided Maxwell for "your offering people sanctification just now...the bidding them say, 'I believe...'
Later he seemed to have become more tolerant
toward instantaneous sanctification, though never
fully at ease with it. As has been noted several times,
Wesley insisted on spiritual growth before and after
any instantaneous experience.

Much has been made by some of the fact that there
is no record of Wesley ever testifying to Christian
perfection in his own life. It is inconceivable that he
could describe it and defend it with out having experienced it. Wesley frequently cautioned against testifying to the experience if one did feel that one was
there. First he felt that it was possible to be mistaken
in one's own conviction that one was in the state of
Christian perfection. Second he felt that, rather than
accomplishing any good, testifying to the experience

might set one up for ridicule and turn people away from the gospel. Third, Wesley feared spiritual pride that could result from making a claim, a pride that would indicate that one was not governed by perfect love. The caution and humility shown here tell us much about Wesley. Unfortunately, many on both sides of the Atlantic were not restricted by any such inhibitions.

Though Wesley spoke and wrote with assurance about the doctrine of Christian perfection he did express some doubts, especially to his brother and best friend, Charles, as late as 1769, thirty-one years after Aldersgate. In a letter to Charles dated 14 May 1768, he wrote:

"But what shall we do? I think it is high time that you and I, at least, should come to a point. Shall we go on asserting perfection against the world? Or shall we quietly let it drop? We really must do one or the other; and I apprehend the sooner the better. What shall we jointly and explicitly maintain, (and recommend to our preachers,) concerning the nature, the time, (now or by and by?). I am weary of intestine war; of preachers quoting one of us against the other. At length, let us fix something for good and all; either the same as formerly, or different from it. [22]

In another letter to Charles, dated 25 March 1772 John wrote:

I find almost all of our preachers, in every circuit, have done with Christian perfection. They say they believe it: but they never preach it; or not once in a quarter. What is to be done? Shall we let it drop, or make a point of it? [23]

These above quotes indicate that thirty years after Aldersgate and forty-three years after Wesley first preached his sermon, *Circumcision of the Heart*, Wesley's doctrine of Christian perfection was in danger of oblivion. Yet, when one goes back to Wesley's original statements of what Christian perfection is, "Loving the Lord our God with all our heart, soul and mind and our neighbor as our selves", there is a beauty and hope in it. It becomes, at the very least, a goal toward which Christians should press, strengthen by the grace of the God who is love. The mechanics of it seem insignificant in the light of its beauty and simplicity. Albert Outler in his book, *Theology in the Wesleyan Spirit*, writes:

I've come to believe that he's got something that all of us need, A view that is as contemporary as transactional analysis (and much more realistic), a doctrine that is truly ecumenical; catholic, evangelical and reformed. This vision of the Christian life (complex in many ways, yet quite simple at its core) might help us toward that renewal of the church that we keep talking about and praying for and are yet denied because of our partisan confusions. [24]

The question for us, then, is where did the doctrine of Christian perfection, as taught by John Wesley, go in Methodism? What became of it?

CHAPTER SIX: THE AMERICANIZATION OF JOHN WESLEY'S DOCTRINE OF CHRISTIAN PERFECTION

As we saw at the close of the last chapter, John Wesley's doctrine of Christian perfection was being taken in directions in the British Isles to which he strongly objected. By exerting the immense power of his personal influence he was able to force people such as Thomas Maxwell, who he saw as perverting his doctrine, out of the Methodist Movement. He was, however, not able to silence such people and their teachings went through out the kingdom and became a part of the theological mix surrounding the doctrine. This was unfortunate because it created confusion in many people's minds as to just what the doctrine really was. Because of this confusion Wesley was credited with teaching things about Christian perfection that he did not teach.

In the hands of the scholarly and cautious Wesley, who very much desired the Methodist movement to remain within the Church of England, the doctrine of Christian perfection was treated with caution and humility. Theologically unsophisticated people such as Maxwell, on the other hand, had none of Wesley's inhibitions. At the hands of such, extravagant claims were made and Christian perfection was preached as an esoteric experience which separated a comparatively small number of the initiated form all other Christian who did not claim the experience or did not claim it in the same form they did.

As seen in the following quote from Wesley's letter to Thomas Maxwell and in, *A Plain Account of Christian Perfection,* and in several sermons and other writings, the doctrine was treated with humility by Wesley. In his letter to Maxwell, Wesley entreated him not to teach the doctrine in such a way as for it to become a wedge to divide Christians one from another. After listing a number of things he did not like about the way Maxwell was preaching Christian perfection, Wesley continued the letter with these words:

> But what I most of all dislike, is your littleness of love to your bretheren, to your own society, your want of union of heart with them, and bowels of mercy toward them; your want of meekness, gentleness, long suffering: your impatience with contradiction; your counting

every man your enemy that reproves you or admonishes you in love; your bigotry, and narrowness of spirit, loving in manner only those who love you; your censoriousness, proneness to think harshly of all who do not exactly agree with you; in one word, your devisive spirit. Indeed I do not believe that any of you want a separation; but you do not enough fear, abhor, and detest it, shuddering at the very though; And all the proceeding tempers tend to it, and gradually prepare you for it. Observe, I tell you before. God grant that you may immediately and effectionately take warning. [1.]

It is obvious from the above quote that Wesley heartily desired that the preaching of the doctrine of Christian perfection not become devisive in the Methodist societies, nor that it would bring about a separation of Methodism from the Church of England.

It becomes obvious as one reads Wesley's writings that he was strongly opposed to anything that would lead to a division in the church and by church he meant his beloved Church of England. He could not accept that the doctrine of Christian perfection as he taught it (being governed by love of God and all persons) could possibly be a devisive influence in the church.

As we have observed, however, in the evangelical revival, in eighteenth century England that came to be known as the Wesleyan Revival, Christian perfection was not always taught as Wesley would have it taught. Christian perfection was indeed a doctrine that could be easily misunderstood and easily corrupted in the wrong hands. In those wrong hands it became esoteric and fanatical with excessive claims and excessive emotionalism. In Wesley's letter to Maxwell, quoted above, it can be seen just how far from Wesley's teachings, Christian perfection was carried in his life time.

Even between the two brothers, John and Charles, there seems to have been differences in understanding and preaching the doctrine. Charles, at times, seemed to have come close to abandoning the doctrine as evidenced in a letter from John to Charles on 9 July 1766.

One word more: Concerning setting perfection too high. That perfection which I believe, I can boldly preach; because I think I see five hundred witnesses of it. Of the perfection you preach, you do not think you see any witnesses at all. Why, then, you must have more courage than me, or you could not persist in preaching it. I wonder, you do not in this article fall in plum with Mr. Whitefield. For do you not, as well as he, ask, "Where are the perfect ones?" I verily believe there are none upon the earth; none dwelling in the body. I cordially assent to this opinion, that there is no such perfection as you describe: At least I never met with an instance of it: and doubt I

ever shall. Therefore I think to set perfection
so high is effectively to renounce it. [2.]

One could wish that John would have elabo-
rated a bit more in this letter as to what he meant by
"setting perfection to high". It would seem he felt
Charles was making excessive claims for the experiences. It would be interesting to know just how much
John and Charles differed at this time concerning
Christian perfection. It is apparent that Charles was
making claims for Christian perfection that could
not be realized and that he was prepared to quit
preaching it because he had never seen an example
of the perfection he was preaching as a possibility.
One cannot help but wonder what Charles' personal
experience with the doctrine had been. Did he experience it? The reference to George Whitefield in
the letter demonstrates that the three major personalities, Whitefield and the Wesley brothers, responsible for the evangelical revival in England, were
not in agreement concerning the cardinal doctrine of
Wesley's theology! There was far from a consensus
concerning the doctrine of Christian perfection even
while the movement was still under the control of
John Wesley.

Wesley, himself, seemed at times, plagued with
doubts concerning the validity of the doctrine. The
fact that he and Charles were not always in agreement on the matter seemed to have greatly troubled
John. In a letter of 12 February 1776 he wrote to
Charles:

I still think, to disbelieve all the professors amounts to a denial of the thing. For if there is no living witness to what we have preached for twenty years. I can not, dare not, preach it any longer. The whole comes to one point: Is there or is there not any instantaneous sanctification between justification and death? I say, yes. You often seem to say, no. What arguments brought you to think so? Perhaps they may convince me too.

Nay; there is one question more, if you allow me there is such a thing: Can one who has attained it fall? Formerly I thought not; but you (with Thomas Walsh and John Jones) convinced me of my mistake. [3.]

This personal note to his brother Charles, thirty years after Aldersgate, does not demonstrate the assuredness we have come to expect from John Wesley as seen in his sermons and other writings. This letter also demonstrates Wesley's willingness to admit to being wrong and his willingness to change his mind on matters of doctrine. He seems to have felt safe in sharing with his younger brother, and best friend, what he could not share with others, a lack of complete assuredness.

It was evidently very important to John that Charles support him in his teaching and preaching on Christian perfection. On 14 May 1768 John wrote in a letter to Charles:

I am at my wit's end with regard to two things, - the Church (Church of England) and Christian perfection. Unless you and I stand in the gap in good earnest, the Methodists will drop them both. Talking will no avail. We must do, or be borne away. Will you set shoulder to shoulder? If so think deeply on this matter, and tell me what can be done. [4.]

The above paragraph from the letter of 14 May 1768 and a paragraph from another letter to Charles a month later on 14 June 1768 in which he wrote:

...Shall we go on in asserting Christian perfection against all the world? Or shall we quietly let it drop? We really must do one or the other and, I apprehend, the sooner the better. [5.]

This letter indicates that Wesley had two major fears for the Methodists in England, first, that they might drop (leave) the Church of England, and second, that they would abandon the doctrine of Christian perfection. It is evident that he also saw another danger for the doctrine of Christian perfection, that in the hands of fanatics it would become a dangerous and divisive doctrine in the church. On all three accounts it seems that Wesley's worst fears were realized in both England and America.

Whether or not Christian perfection was to be preached in Methodism and if so, how, was not a matter easily settled. We have seen that Wesley was concerned that his preachers were all but ignoring the doctrine. In his book, *Christian Perfection and American Methodism,* John L. Peters quotes a contemporary of Wesley's, John Hampson, writing about Christian perfection saying this:

> For many years the shibboleth of Methodism... Perfectionists and Anti-Perfectionists were grand divisions... The wags laughed merrily at the witnesses...Even their bretheren eyed them askance, and set a mark upon them: while the Calvinian Methodists in song and madrigals and heroics, alternately vented their mirth and their indignation.[6.]

Since Hamson had a falling out with Wesley over the Trust Deeds there may well have been some bias in the above statement, but there is little question that while Wesley was still alive the doctrine of Christian perfection, as Wesley taught it, was far from being fully accepted by all Methodists.

We cannot leave the doctrine of Christian perfection in England with out at least a mention of the Rev. John Fletcher (1729-1785). Fletcher is important at this point because his writings were influential in both England and America. Fletcher was born in Switzerland of French Huguenot parents. He arrived in England in 1752 and became a Church of England priest. He was rector at Madeley when he and John Wesley became close friends. They developed a deep and abiding appreciation for each other. The appreciation for Fletcher on Wesley's part was so great that Fletcher was Wesley's choice to succeed him as leader of the Methodist societies. That was not to be since Fletcher preceded Wesley in death.

Fletcher seems to have been as zealous as Wesley had been in seeking a closer relationship with God. They followed very similar paths in coming to their views on Christian perfection. Fletcher was an able theologian and became Wesley's champion in his conflicts with Calvinists, within and without the Methodist movement. Thomas A. Langford says of Fletcher, "Through his writings, Fletcher became the spokesperson and the systematizer of the positions Wesley had taken." [7] Fletcher's major work was, *"Checks to Antimonianism."* (Antimonianism is the teaching that since one is saved by grace, not works, one is no longer under the moral law and is free to break the law with out fear of retribution.) Fletcher listed five checks, the last one dealing with the doctrine of Christian perfection. Langford, in speaking of the five checks, especially the last one writes."

There were some new suggestions, such as the relationship of sanctification to the experience of Jesus' disciples at Pentecost (in the fifth check) the emphasis on the instantaneous event of sanctification, and the use of dispensational categories. In these ways Fletcher both reinforced and went beyond Wesley's theological work. [8]

Fletcher did go beyond Wesley in equating the Pentecostal experience with sanctification. This was later to become an integral aspect of the teaching of sanctification in the American holiness movement. This equating of Pentecost and sanctification is not to be found in the writings of John Wesley. We have also seen, in Wesley's letters to his brother Charles, that the issue, of instantaneous versus growth sanctification, never seemed to be quite settled. When Wesley did allow for an instantaneous sanctification he also insisted that spiritual growth was to continue. John Fletcher became known as the father of Methodist theology and his influence was strong in both England and America.

Wesley's Doctrine of Christian Perfection in Colonial America:

Methodism first appeared in America in the person of George Whitefield, a close personal friend of Wesley's, (part of the time) and a member of the original Oxford group. Whitefield was the person who introduced Wesley to field preaching, something that originally appalled Wesley. It was his mother, Susanna, who pointed out to him that if it was good enough for Jesus it ought to be good enough for him. Whitefield, however, had strong Calvinistic leanings and was not in accord with Wesley concerning Christian perfection. Whitefield was an excellent preacher and he drew great crowds in colonial America. He worked closely with the New England Calvinists in what has come to be known as the "Second Great Awakening." Though Whitefield and Wesley worked together in England in the very early days of the evangelical revival their theological disagreements separated Whitefield from Methodism and Methodism did not gain a foot old in America because of Whitefield's work. Whitefield was not an organizer as was Wesley. Whitefield did not organize and supervise societies and classes. He was a sower who went forth to sow and as a result he left no movement behind to conserve his harvest.

Another factor which hindered the growth of Methodism in the colonies was that John Wesley openly expressed his dismay with the American colonists for their wanting to separate from the mother country. This caused some real resentment towards Methodism in the American colonies.

For the above mentioned reasons Methodism was slow to gain a foothold in America prior to the American revolution. When Methodism was introduced into the American Colonies it was the result of lay Methodists immigrating from England and Ireland, who with out the help of clergy, organized societies and classes, patterned after those in the British Isles.

Robert Strawbridge established the first Methodist society in Maryland in the mid 1760s. Barbara Heck was instrumental in getting a Methodist society established in New York City at about the same time. As more Methodists immigrated to America, more societies were established and Methodism began to grow. At the request of these societies, Wesley sent two lay preachers, Robert Boardman and Joseph Pilmore to the American colonies in 1769.

In 1771 Wesley sent Francis Asbury to America. Asbury did not return to England when the colonists revolted. His life was in danger at times and he had to hide out for awhile. Wesley had taken a strong and vocal stance against the separation of the American colonies from England causing the Methodists to be suspected of being Tories. (those sympathetic to the British cause)

In 1784, following the successful conclusion (from the American perspective) of the Revolutionary war, Wesley sent the Rev. Thomas Coke to America. Wesley's plan was that Thomas coke and Francis Asbury were to become joint superintendents of the Methodists in America. In 1784, at the famous Christmas Conference the Methodist Episcopal Church was formed as separate from the Church of England and Thomas Coke and Francis Asbury were elected its first two bishops. The new bishops could not have been more different. Asbury was a lay preacher with out formal education. At the Christmas Conference he was ordained a deacon and an elder on the same day and consecrated as a bishop on the next day. He would not act as a superintendent appointed by Wesley in England, and would only serve if elected by Americans. Though born in England he was very adaptable to the American scene.

Thomas Coke on the other hand was an ordained priest in the Church of England. He was Oxford educated with B.A., M.A. and a Doctor of Civil Law degree. He had at one time been the Mayor of his home town of Brecon in Wales. Wesley had appointed him as superintendent of the London District in 1782. We will discuss the difference between these two bishops and what those differences meant to American Methodism in a later chapter.

Wesley was not entirely happy with what was going on in Methodism in America. He was opposed to the separation of the colonies from England, he was opposed to the separation of Methodism from the Church of England and he was very opposed to Coke and Asbury assuming the title Bishop. Following the Revolutionary War, American Methodists still revered Wesley but they were out from under his control and intent on running their own affairs. To be perfectly fair, the Americans had a much clearer picture of what was going on in America that did John Wesley. An example of the fact that American Methodists were out from under Wesley's control is the rejection of the worship book Wesley had prepared for the American Methodists, *The Sunday Service for the Methodists in North America*. The service was almost never used by the American Methodists from the beginning and was completely lost to use on the expanding frontier. More will be said concerning this deviation from Wesley's theology of church and worship in a later chapter.

Though Wesley was not allowed to exert any authority over American Methodism as to structure and liturgy, he was looked upon by Americans with great respect and affection. In matters of doctrine he was the final authority. The deviations from Wesley's theology that this author finds as a result of the influence of the American frontier were not deliberate. Through Wesley's writings and those of John Fletcher and Adam Clark, the Wesleyan doctrine of

Christian perfection came to America and was never intentionally discarded. The changes were real but unintentional. Thomas Langford writes of Francis Asbury:

> Asbury's contribution to (American Methodism) was enormous; he was director and example, the overseer and chief advocate of the movement. But he did not make a theological contribution beyond preserving, by reiteration, the chief themes of Wesley [9.]

Following the creation of the new nation, Americans began to move westward toward and then beyond the Allegheny Mountains. Bishop Asbury devised a unique system of circuits which were to be ridden by preachers between sessions of Annual conference, at which time they would be either reassigned or assigned to another circuit. These circuit riders spent a great deal of their lives on horseback, sleeping in settler's cabins or in the open and preaching at every opportunity in all kinds of places, taverns, cabins and in the open. They would gather their converts into classes and appoint class leaders then ride on to do it over and over. If it was a comparatively small circuit they would come by several times a year; if it was a larger circuit fewer times. The circuit system was uniquely adaptable to a frontier that was ever in a state of flux. As the population flowed westward the circuits were expanded and new circuits created. The circuit riders kept Methodism on the growing edge of the nation.

By European standards and by the standards of Colonial America many of these westward moving pioneers were barely civilized. Illiteracy, lawlessness, drunkenness and brawling were very much a part of life on the frontier in the late eighteenth and early nineteenth centuries. In his autobiography, Peter Cartwright, one of the better known Methodist circuit riders, describes the frontier community in which he was brought up.

> Logan county (Kentucky) when my father moved to it was called "Rogues' Harbor". Here many refugees, from almost all parts of the Union, fled to escape justice or punishment; for although there was law, yet it could not be executed, and it was a desperate state of society. Murderers, horse thieves, highway robbers and counterfeiters fled here till they actually formed a majority. [10].

Cartwright then speaks of the "honest and civil part of the citizens" organizing themselves to drive the less desirable element of the citizenry out, at first they were unsuccessful but Cartwright continues.

> The Regulators rallied again, hunted, killed and lynched many of the rouges, till several of them fled and left for parts unknown. Many lives were lost on both sides, to the great scandal of civilized people. This is but a partial view of the frontier life. [11.]

Undoubtedly this was, as Cartwright wrote, a partial view of the frontier and not representative of the best people moving westward to build new homes and new lives. But we do have enough collaborating testimony from other writers to know that frontier society tended to be crude and rude.

What was needed most in frontier society was not Wesley's doctrine of Christian perfection, but a solid converting experience. What the early Methodist circuit riders preached to the frontier people was a simple gospel of "be saved or be dammed". The circuit riders did not have time to lead people from justification to a hungering after Christian perfection. The job of the circuit rider, as time and energy allowed, was to save as many people from "hell fire" as possible, and to organize them into classes for prayer and study. These men burned themselves out doing just that. As the population grew most of these classes became Churches. All of this is not to say that a new and more pious life was not demanded of the converts. They were expected to grow in grace. Nor is it to say that the circuit riders completely abandoned the Wesleyan doctrine of Christian perfection. They preached a mangled version of it.

Peter Cartwright wrote of an incident at the Breckenridge circuit camp meeting in 1813, "Many at this meeting sought and obtained the blessing of sanctification." He goes on then to write of a Sister S. and her experience of sanctification.

> She had long sought the blessing of perfect love,...Her whole soul was in an agony for

that blessing, and it seemed at times to her that she could almost lay hold, and claim the promise, but she said her slaves would seem to step right in between her and her savior, and prevent its reception; but while on her knees and struggling as in a great agony for a clean heart, she then and there covenanted with the Lord, if he would give her the blessing, she would give up her slaves and set them free. She said this covenant had hardly been made one moment, when God filled her soul with such an overwhelming sense of Divine love, that she did not really know whether she was in or out of her body. She rose from her knees, and proclaimed to listening hundreds that she had obtained the blessing, and also the terms on which she had obtained it. She went through the vast crowd with shouts of joy, and exhorted all to taste and see that the Lord was gracious, and such a power attended her words that hundreds fell to the ground, and scores of souls were happily born into the kingdom of God that afternoon and during the night. Shortly after this they set their slaves free, and the end of that family was peace. [12.]

This and many other references that could be cited from Cartwright's writings, and those of other circuit riders of the era, indicate that Christian perfection or sanctification was preached and sought after on the frontier. The above quote from Cartwright demonstrates that it was preached as something to be arrived at instantaneously through an act of faith. Wesley came to believe that it could be arrived at in an instant. But Wesley believed that the usual time for coming into the experience was at the moment of death, after a lifetime of spiritual growth. On the frontier in the 19th century the instantaneous approach came to be the norm.

A most interesting aspect of Cartwright's story is the deal the woman made with God, the trade of her slaves for the experience of sanctification. One also wonders what Wesley's reaction would have been to the woman's ecstatic manifestation.

Though the preaching of Christian perfection never disappeared from the frontier it was emphasized less and less. When it was preached and experienced it was in a different form than which Wesley would have taught, and with a different purpose than Wesley's. John L. Peters in his book, *Christian Perfection and American Methodism,* writes:

> Neverthe less, it should not be assumed that the primary doctrine of the Methodist Episcopal Church during its first two decades was entire sanctification. Christian perfection was a respected but not a dominate feature of the preaching of this period. A review of sermon topics, conference reports, and early biographies clearly indicate that fact. It is entirely possible to read some thoroughly trustworthy and comprehensive accounts of these early

years without supposing that perfection was more than an incidental feature.[13.]

The Conference of 1812 voted to remove the Doctrinal Tracts from the Discipline and to publish them in another volume. This was done for size and convenience. The Doctrinal Tracts contained Wesley's *A Plain Account of Christian Perfection,* and other doctrinal statements. It was planned that a separate volume containing the Doctrinal Tracts was to be published immediately and circulated throughout the church. What happened was that the volume containing the Doctrinal Tracts did not appear for twenty years, until 1832. The practical result of this long delay was to remove the doctrine of Christian perfection from authorized and circulated material for a generation.

The Pastoral Address delivered to the 1832 General Conference raised and answered this question:

> Why...have we so few living witnesses that the blood of Jesus cleans from all sin...Among primitive Methodists, the experience of this high attainment in religion may justly be said to have been common; now a profession of it is rarely to be met among us.[14]

Peters goes on to say:

> The issues of the Methodist Magazine and Quarterly Review from 1830 to 1840 give the

impression that this doctrine was of well nigh esoteric nature - nor seriously questioned nor generally preached. Occasional articles expounding it and defending it - usually in strictest Wesleyan terms - but Christian perfection seems not to have been a vital ingredient in general Methodist thought and life during this period. Between 1836 and 1840 not one article on the subject appeared in the Quarterly Review.[15]

It would not be correct to assume from this fact that the teaching and preaching of the doctrine of Christian perfection was entirely ignored in American Methodism during the first half of the nineteenth century. In 1825 a Methodist preacher by the name of Timothy Merritt had published a small volume titled, The *Christian Manual, A Treatise on Christian Perfection*. It was said of Merritt, "Christian perfection was his favorite theme, and he was a living example of it."[16]

In 1826 Nathan Bang, head of the Methodist Book Concern, and one of American Methodism's first real scholars, and probably its first historian, wrote a series of articles suggesting a course of study for young ministers. This series of articles was published as,*Letters to Young Ministers of the Gospel, on the Importance and Method of Study*. Under Christian Theology Bangs suggested:

On the doctrines of Repentance, Justification, Sanctification, you can find no authors who have illustrated those subjects with greater clearness and accuracy than Wesley and Fletcher.

That the young circuit riders took seriously Bang's suggestions for study seems doubtful judging from the samples of their preaching available to us. As Peters has pointed out there was a real lack of emphasis on the doctrine of Christian perfection or Holiness as it was coming to be called in America.

Resurgence of Interest In The Doctrine:

It was not the frontier circuit riders or even the few scholars in American Methodism in the mid-nineteenth century who brought about a renewed interest in the doctrine of Christian perfection. It was a lay movement. And, what is more astounding, considering the time, it was a movement in which women played the key role.

In 1835 in New York City, the women of the Allen Street and the Mulberry Street Methodist churches, under the leadership of Phoebe (Mrs. W.C.) Palmer and her sister, Mrs. Sarah Langford, began the Tuesday Meetings for the Promotion of Holiness. These meetings lasted for over sixty years![17] For the first four years the meetings were open to women only, but then they were opened up to men as well. Nathan Bangs attended for a time and at least two other ministers who were later to become bishops.

Phoebe Palmer is important to the history of the Methodism especially and to Protestantism in general for two reasons. First, she enlarged the role of woman in religion by moving it beyond the concept of the pious woman who dabbed in religion while maintaining as her first responsibility, her home, her children and her husband. Because of financial security (her husband was a successful physician) she was able to move into the ranks of evangelist and theologian. Second, she is important for just that reason; she is credited with having been instrumental in twenty-five thousand conversions in America and England. She is best known, however, as the theologian of a type of holiness teaching, that for a time in America was considered orthodox Methodist theology, though it little resembled Wesley's teaching on the subject. She promoted her brand of holiness through the Tuesday Meetings, in numerous articles, in her preaching, and in the periodical, Guide to Holiness, which she and her husband purchased and published.

Though Phoebe gave impetus to a leadership role for women in American Protestantism she would not have considered herself a feminist. That was not her battle, at least consciously. She believed that there were cases in which God called certain women to take an active role in moving the religious scene toward the millennium. She interpreted the death of two of her six children as God's way of telling her that she should put God first in her life and devote more of her time and energy to God's work. This has a sick sound to it, but one is reminded of the letter John Wesley wrote to his sister, Hetty at the death of the last of her several children in which he said that the death was a blessing in that she was now free to devote more time and energy to God's work. Apparently, neither Wesley or Phoebe saw the raising of children in a wholesome, Christian home to be God's work! And, yet they were both raised in such homes. Phoebe's father had been converted under the preaching of John Wesley and family devotions and church attendance were very much a part of her childhood. She seems to have been unable to give a date for her conversion (justification). This was not true of her experience of entire sanctification (Christian perfection). That according to her testimony took place on 26 July 1837. Her sister, Sarah Langford, had claimed the experience two years earlier at 2:00 p.m. on 21 May 1835. After Phoebe claimed the experience she and Sarah began the famous Tuesday Meetings for the Promotion of Holiness, These meetings were to become the real molding force of the doctrine of Christian perfection or sanctification in American Methodism. Though Phoebe Palmer molded Methodist theology as it related to the paramount Wesleyan doctrine, there were others who shared most of her views. Some of these were more scholarly in their approaches. But, it was Phoebe Palmer who did as much as anyone to Americanize Wesley's doctrine of Christian perfection, sometimes called sanctification, but more often in Phoebe's circles, called holiness.

The distinctive marks of this doctrine, as a result of its Americanization at the hands of Palmer and others, that distinguished it from the doctrine as taught by John Wesley were, first, the emphasis on the instantaneous aspect of the experience. He did allow for it. But, as we have seen from his letters to his brother Charles, well into the Wesleyan revival, he was still wrestling with this issue. Wesley's emphasis was on constant growth and maturing spiritually, from justification until death, which he said on several occasions, was the usual time of perfection. The doctrine was preached in America as a "second definite work of grace". As we saw in the chapter on grace, Wesley did not see grace as something that God bestows on us, rather grace is God himself, the God who is love, interacting with us in a loving relationship. This concept would seem to render "a second definite work of Grace" or "the second blessing" unnecessary. Wesley did not seem to see Christian perfection as necessary to salvation, but rather as salvation's goal. Phoebe taught that if one did not enter into the "second definite work of grace" one would lose the first.

Second. Wesley spoke of the experience in Christological terms. One was to seek to become Christ like by yielding ones will to God following the example of Christ. In mid-nineteenth century America holiness is spoken of in pneumenological terms. When one was sanctified one was "filled with the Holy Spirit". The experience was often spoken of as "the baptism of the Holy Spirit". For Palmer and her followers the purpose of the experience was power, the power of the Holy Spirit in one's life. The American holiness movement placed a strong emphasis on The Power of the Holy Spirit and the gifts of the Spirit, prophesy, healing, exhorting and teaching.

Wesley, on the other hand, emphasized the fruits of the Spirit, patience, faithfulness, gentleness, kindness, love and purity. For Wesley, Christian perfection was a means to the end of perfect love of God and for the entire human race. That kind of love was the impetus of a strong social emphasis in Wesley's thought. Much of the social emphasis was lost to individualism in the Americanization of the doctrine. Feeling was very important in Palmer's brand of holiness; emotions ran high in the Tuesday Meetings. The experience came with ecstatic manifestations. As well as seeing the experience in Pentecostal terms, as being filled with the Holy Spirit, Palmer also tended to find its roots in the Old Testament sacrificial system. One put one's self, one's life entirely on the alter, a sacrifice with out blemish (no holding back). It was an intentional act that one committed on the faith that God would reward one with the experience of holiness. As the words of the old gospel song ask:

Is your all on the altar of sacrifice laid?
Your heart does the Spirit posses?

Wesley drew from the catholic roots, the early church fathers, monastic writers, Catholic mystics, German pietists and English mystics. He was conversant with the spiritual literature of the ages. Phoebe Palmer and her followers saw holiness as the Pentecostal experience, an experience one simply appropriated by faith.

This approach came to be known, among Methodist theologians, as the "short way" as opposed to what Nathan Bangs called Wesley's "long way", a life time of spiritual maturing.

It might seem that an inordinate amount of space has been devoted to Phoebe Palmer, but phoebe Palmer was probably the person most responsible for the Americanization of Wesley's doctrine of Christian perfection. Wesley's doctrine as modified by Phoebe and her followers was what was preached on the frontier where it was accompanied by even more excess, and subjected to even more change. Phoebe Palmer's version of Christian perfection (holiness) became the pet doctrine of most of the groups that separated themselves from the Methodist Episcopal Church in the nineteenth century. These groups made the preaching of an esoteric, individualistic, highly charged emotional holiness their reason for being.

That John Wesley would have claimed responsibly for the doctrine as preached by Phoebe Palmer and her followers and on the American frontier (when it was preached there) seems very doubtful. Wesley's worst fears for the doctrine were realized on the frontier.

It is probably fair to say that the doctrine of Christian perfection, as understood and taught by John Wesley, was the most distinctive feature of Wesleyan theology. It also seems accurate to say that no aspect of Wesley's theology suffered more violence and became less recognizable in America and on the American frontier in the nineteenth century.

CHAPTER SEVEN: THE AMERICANIZATION OF JOHN WESLEY'S THEOLOGY OF SACRAMENTS AND WORSHIP

I t is a given that one's mode of worship reflects one's theology. One's doctrines of church and sacraments will determine the forms of worship to which one subscribes. This was certainly true of Wesley, who, as has been noted earlier, saw the Church of England "as the most scriptural national church in the world". "I therefore" he continued, "not only assent to all the doctrines, but observe all the rubrics in the Liturgy; and that with all possible exactness, even at the peril of my life." [1] This was written over sixty years after his ordination.

When one observes what came to be considered worship in the Methodist Episcopal Church in the mid-nineteenth century, one is forced to wonder what happened to Wesley's influence on American Methodism.

To understand what happened it is necessary to understand the American mindset at that time in history.

Following the successful outcome of the War for Independence, a disastrous outcome from Wesley's point of view, Wesley who was always a pragmatist, bowed to the facts. In order to keep American Methodists under his influence he did two things. First, he sent Dr. Thomas Coke, an Anglican clergyman, active in the Methodists societies in England, to be a superintendent of the American societies in America. Coke was also, at Wesley's instruction, to appoint Francis Asbury, a lay preacher, who Wesley had sent over earlier, to be another superintendent to share in the administrative load. Asbury had been sent to America previous to the War for Independence. Asbury had elected to remain in America during the war, casting his lot with the colonists. Because of Wesley's outspoken criticism of the American rebellion, Asbury as his appointee, was suspected as to his loyalty to the American cause, and had to be hidden during the war to protect his life.

Second, to maintain his influence over American Methodism, Wesley sent to America, with Thomas Coke, a number of printed but unbound copies of a worship book titled, *The Sunday Service of the Methodists of North America.* They were sent unbound to avoid a duty on bound books. They were to be bound in America. With that service book, Wesley sent a letter by Coke, to American Methodists, dated 10 September 1784 stating in part:

> I have prepared a Liturgy little differing from that of the Church of England (I think the best constituted National Church in the world), which I advise all the traveling preachers to use on the Lord's day in all the congregations, reading the litany only on Wednesdays and Fridays, and praying extempore on all other days. I also advise the elders to administer the Supper of the Lord on every Lord's day. [2]

What actually did happen in North America was something quite different than Wesley had envisioned. Wesley did seem to understand that, Americans were free from control by the British government, thus they were free from England's state church as well. He saw that they were indeed free, even compelled by circumstances, to become a church. What he didn't seem to understand was that he had little or no administrative control over American Methodists. Wesley finished his letter of 10 September 1784, which introduced, *The Sunday Service of the Methodists of North America*, with this paragraph:

> As our American brethren are now totally disentangled from both The State, and from

the English Hierarchy, we dare not entangle
them again either with one or the other. They
are now free to follow the scriptures and the
primitive church. And to stand fast in that
liberty wherewith God has so strangely made
them free. [3]

Wesley was loved and revered by American
Methodists, but following the Revolutionary War,
his instructions were no longer followed to any great
extent. His American children affectionately referred
to him as "Old Daddy Wesley", but like many children, they did not listen to Old Daddy.

At the famed Baltimore Christmas Conference
of 1784, the Methodist Episcopal Church was organized, separate from the Church of England. At
that conference Francis Asbury refused to become
a superintendent, appointed by Wesley in England.
He would become a superintendent only if elected by
the American Methodist preachers. This was done.
Both Coke and Asbury were elected bishops not
superintendents.

As was noted earlier, Francis Asbury was
ordained a deacon on one day and an elder on the next
and consecrated a bishop the same day along with
Thomas Coke. Wesley was furious with Coke and
Asbury for assuming the title of bishops. His letter of
reprimand of 20 September 1788 was scathing. The
brief letter is worth quoting in its entirety because it
demonstrates that Wesley, nearly four years after the
Methodist Episcopal Church of North America had
been established, still believed that he had control-

ling influence over American Methodism. It clearly shows how little Wesley understood the American mind. The lack of response to the letter also shows how little impressed were American Methodists by his claim to authority over them.

To the Rev. Francis Asbury, London, 10 September 1788

There is indeed a wide difference between the relation where in you stand to the Americans, and the relation wherein I stand to all the Methodists. You are elder brother of the American Methodists: I am, under God, the father of the whole family. Therefore, I naturally care for you all; for the supplies Dr. Coke provides for you, he could not provide if it were not for me, - were it not that I not only permit him to collect, but also support him in doing so.

But in one point, my dear brother, I am a little afraid, both the Doctor and you differ from me. I study to be little; you study to be great. I creep; you strut along. I found a school; you found a college! Nay, and call it after your own names! O, beware, do not seek to be something. Let me be nothing, and Christ be all in all!

One instance of all this, of your greatness, has given me great concern. How can you, how dare you, suffer yourself, to be called a Bishop! Let the Presbyterians do what they please, but let the Methodists know their calling better.

Thus my dear Franky, I have told you all that is in my heart. And let this, when I am no more seen, bear witness how sincerely I am, Your affectionate friend and brother.[4]

In passing it is interesting to note that Wesley used as the main foundation for his rationalization for ordaining ministers for the work in America that, the terms presbyter and bishop were synonymous in the primitive church. What is more striking about the letter, however, is the disregard with which it was received. The title bishop continued to be used in American Methodism. Cokesbury College burned to the ground twice and eventually went out of existence, but certainly not because of anything Wesley had to say about it. The letter also indicates, again, how little Wesley understood the American situation.

With the title Bishop, Asbury assumed almost absolute control over the ministers of the new church. In spite of Wesley's reservations, Coke and Asbury were indeed bishops in name and function.

Coke and Asbury were men of very different temperament and background. Asbury was willing and eager to plow straight ahead, fashioning a new and strikingly different episcopal church in America. Coke, on the other hand, shared more of Wesley's reservation about a complete break with the Church of England. Coke, apparently, would like to have slowed down, if not actually reversed Asbury's headlong dash away from Methodism's Anglican roots.

During the Christmas Conference in Baltimore in 1784, at which The Methodist Episcopal Church was instituted, two Protestant Episcopal rectors, John Andrews and William West invited Asbury and Coke to tea. At this tea, Andrews and West tried to dissuade Coke and Asbury from forming a separate church. They suggested that special bishops might be provided for the Methodists, by the Church of England. The tea changed no one's mind, least of all Asbury's. At any rate it was already too late. "The former Anglicans were themselves, throughout the 1790's in the protracted and difficult process of forming a new Protestant Episcopal Church in the United States."[5] Two episcopal churches were being formed in America by people whose roots were in the Church of England.

"In 1787 William White, who was to become a bishop in the Protestant Episcopal Church, sought while visiting in England, to have conversations with John and Charles Wesley, about the issue of keeping the American children of Anglicanism together in one church. He did talk with Charles. Nothing came of this effort." [6] Apparently William White, believed the Wesley brothers to have more influence in America than they actually had. The attempt to keep the children of Anglicanism together in one church was not one sided. In 1791 Coke approached White and Seabury, by then bishops in the new Protestant Episcopal Church. He proposed reunion on the basis of episcopal ordination for himself and Francis Asbury. Before Coke could receive a reply from his letter to White he was called back to England by the death of John Wesley. Coke wrote to Bishop Seabury on 14 May 1791 with the same proposal. Again nothing came of it.

There was yet another attempt by a Protestant Episcopal Bishop, James Madison of Virginia to form a basis for union. His proposal was rejected by, the lower house of the General Convention of the Protestant Episcopal Church. The proposal apparently did not make its way to the Methodists, who would have undoubtedly rejected it. Was the outcome of two episcopal churches in America inevitable? The answer is probably, yes. Norwood raises and answers that question in his book, *The Story of American Methodism*:

> Did separation of Anglicans and Methodists (in America) thus take place by the skin of the teeth? Probably the decision was inevitable in spite of possible delays and compromises. The forces at work in American Christianity were such as to push the two groups, for the time being, farther apart. The equivocal position of John Wesley, the unwillingness of Anglican authorities to act, the impatience of American leaders, and the powerful revivalism, and the pressure toward pluralism in American religion conspired to separate the Methodists and Episcopalians. The forces, perhaps ultimately more deeply rooted, which would tend to bring them together were for the time being submerged. [7]

In American Methodism immediately after the Revolutionary War, there were two very distinct and very different spirits at work, one represented by Francis Asbury, the other by Thomas Coke. Asbury was originally unaware of Cokes efforts at union with the Protestant Episcopal Church. When Asbury did become aware of those efforts he was angry with his Episcopal colleague, and succeeded in having him pretty much removed from his duties in America. Asbury, though English by birth, had chosen to cast his lot with the American Colonists. He had stayed in America during the war. Because of the very strong stand Wesley had taken against American Independence, Asbury, as Wesley's appointee, was suspect as to his loyalties to the American cause. Asbury was well suited to become an American. He was one of Wesley's lay preachers, without formal education. He was not from the English upper classes. Though he was to be an almost absolute authoritarian in his role as bishop, he was not about to submit to authority from England, even that of John Wesley. Asbury did not share Wesley's or Coke's deep love for the Church of England, nor for its rituals and doctrines. Asbury could easily slip into the American mind set.

Thomas Coke, on the other hand, was quite a different type. He was an ordained priest in the Church of England. He held an earned doctorate. He shared Wesley's love for the Church of England and did not easily leave it, even to become a bishop in a new church. As has been noted, Coke, worked for union between the Methodists and the Protestant

Episcopal; Church, which was more nearly, the successor of the Church of England in America. It was Thomas Coke who brought the service book from Wesley to American Methodists with instructions that this be the worship book for American Methodists. Coke seems to have believed that since the book came from Wesley's hands it would be readily acceptable to Methodists in America. That was not to be the case.

John Wesley said of, *The Sunday Service of the United Methodist in North America*, that it was an abridgment of The Book of Common Prayer of the Church of England. It was also quite similar to the prayer book of the new Protestant Episcopal Church in America. For Coke and Wesley the expectation was, that the Methodists, though they could no longer be part of the Church of England would at least remain within the Anglican family of churches. This was not to be. History shows us that it was the spirit, personified in Asbury, that was to win out in American Methodism. In reading this part of the manuscript to Eva, my very patient wife, she remarked, "Thus we ended up being an Asbury church rather than a Coke church." That observation summed up in one sentence what I have been trying to say in several paragraphs.

Coke seems to have been, almost as lacking in an understanding of the situation in America, as was Wesley. From one of his many visits to England, Coke, was sent, by Wesley back to America, with instructions for the American Methodists to gather in a conference the following May and to accept

Richard Whatcoat, as a third superintendent (bishop). The Americans had already selected a different date and were not about to change it, nor were they ready to accept Richard Whatcoat as a third superinten-dent from Wesley. On this incident and its outcome, Frederick Norwood writes:

> Coke got his fingers burned on this episode, because he had incautiously brought Wesley's instructions under the assump-tion that they would be followed explicitly. He was forced to agree that he would not attempt to administer American affairs when he was in Europe. By 1880 the estrangement had gone so far, as recorded in the Journal of the General Conference, 'Dr. Coke, at the request of the British, and by consent of our General Conference, resides in Europe. He is not to exercise the office of superintendent among us, in the United States, until he be recalled by the General Conference, or by all the Annual Conferences respectively.' [8]

The above action by the General Conference shows how wide the rift had become between Wesley and the American Methodists in matters of administration. Thus American Methodism went in a very different direction than Wesley had envisioned. At no point did American Methodism depart from Wesley more than in matters of worship.

The Sunday Worship of the Methodists in North America, sent by Wesley for use by the Methodists in America, was almost immediately ignored by the Americans. In passing, one can only wonder how long the book had been in preparation. Obviously it was not hastily compiled. One is led to believe that Wesley had anticipated the formation of the new church long before it occurred. There was no need, at the time, for such a book for the English Methodists, since they were still expected to attend the Church of England for the Sacraments. British Methodists met in chapels or in meeting houses for their preaching services, at hours that did not conflict with the services at the parish church.

The situation was much different in America. The worship Wesley, had suggested for the Americans did not fit, certainly not on the frontier. American Methodism developed in the pluralism of a number of denominations with whom they sometimes competed, and with whom they sometimes cooperated, such as in revivals and camp meetings.

What resulted from this mixing was a sort of American folk religion in which it was difficult to tell one denomination's worship from another's. The Lutherans and Episcopalians, and of course the Roman Catholics did not become a part of the folk religion. The Methodists, Presbyterians, Baptists, and Campbellites were similar enough in their worship to be able to work together in camp meetings and revivals. The camp meetings and revivals impacted heavily on Protestant worship in America.

What came to be the norm in worship for American Methodists was not dissimilar from the preaching services that Wesley and his lay preachers conducted in England, in their chapels and preaching houses, which, according to Wesley, were to be in addition to attendance at the Church of England services for the sacraments.

Methodist worship came to center, not on the Lord's Supper, but on the preaching. This was demonstrated in Church architecture with the pulpit, not the altar, at the center of the chancel. The chancel was often referred to as the platform and the nave as the auditorium, a far cry from Wesley's vision for American Methodists!

The worship style that developed on the frontier and which lasted after the frontier ended was very similar among Protestants of most denominations, except Lutherans and Episcopalians. It was a free style of worship interspersed, with much congregational singing, the reading of a scripture passage, long extemporary prayers and at least a half hour sermon. The exception was the quarterly communion service, which was done with a minimum of liturgy so that it did not overly interfere with the normal flow of the service in which preaching was the prominent feature.

Raymond George in an article, titled, *Sunday Service 1784*, in Doxology, Journal of the order of St. Luke in the United Methodist Church, concerning its use in American Methodism, wrote:

> In America, none of this lasted long. Evening prayer sank almost without a trace, or was replaced by a simple Free Church type of preaching service, called by its detractors a

hymn-sandwich. In most churches much the same thing happened to the morning service, though this sometimes retained traces of Morning Prayer, such as the occasional use of psalms or canticles as well as the two lessons, a sort of greatly mangled Matins. This development was due to assimilation of the simple preaching services which Wesley had held at 5 a.m. and 5 p.m. outside church hours. [9]

One of the most significant departures from Wesley's instructions pertaining to the sacrament of the Lord's Supper was the frequency with which it was observed. Wesley advocated it be administered every Lord's Day. The form for Holy Communion was pretty much as prescribed in Wesley's service book. What did change was the frequency of the sacrament, going from fifty-two times a year to four. Monthly Communion came later.

The main factor contributing to the infrequency of Holy Communion, that came to be the norm in American Methodism, had its origin on the frontier. Most of the time there was no ordained minister available to celebrate the sacrament. The circuit riding minister could only meet with the Methodists of a given area two to four times a year. Some of the circuit riders were not ordained but on probation, that is, they were serving a probationary period to see if they were cut out for ordination. One of the criteria was, had they survived!

These influences, a desire to be free from English domination, religious pluralism, revivalism and emotionalism, and the circuit riding system, conspired to put American Methodism well within the free church tradition. When one considers, that Wesley's original reason for ordaining men to ministry was that American Methodists would have access to the Lord's Supper, it seems ironic that the Americans held the sacrament in such low regard.

Not only did American Methodism, on the frontier, relegate Holy Communion to a quarterly observance, it also changed the meaning of the sacrament. In the American folk religion, that we have said resulted from the melding of theologies and practices between the various religious groups on the frontier, Holy Communion became little more than a memorail. This was pretty much the understanding of the sacrament that Methodism fostered until recently. As late as 1956, Methodist Bishop, John M. Moore could write the following concerning consubstantiation, after having done away with transubstantiation:

> The miraculous element in this sacrament could not be possible without miracle working power in the ministerial order of bishop and priest. The doctrine of an imperialistic, sacerdotal ministry, transmitted from the apostles and by the apostles to bishops, and from them to elders or priests, preceded and produced the doctrine of the presence of Jesus Christ in the physical elements of the sacrament. [10]

In the above quote, Moore, in speaking of the real presence of Jesus Christ in the sacrament, actually calls it magic and superstition. He seems to make no allowance for God's action in the sacrament. He also states that his understanding of the sacrament has been the norm in Methodism. And therein lies the problem!

J. Earnest Rattenbury, in his book, *Wesley's Legacy in the World*, quotes a man by the name of Riggs, author of *The Churchmanship of John Wesley*, as saying that: the Wesley before Aldersgate was not the same man as after Aldersgate.

> Riggs claim that Wesley's life was divided into two distinct and in many respects, sharply contrasting periods, the period preceding and the period following the spring of 1738. Prior to 1738 he was a strict High Churchman, but the experience of May 24th "ended his High Church style of life. Here began his life as an evangelist and a church revivalist." There was a transition period, but by 1745-1746 the transition not to Low Church but to a Broad Church position was complete.

Rattenbury, on the other hand, claims that:

> There is no greater mistake than to suppose that Wesley ceased to be a High Churchman after 1738. The popular argument that Wesley before and after 1738 were two different men with different views, is a modern Methodist myth which serious investigation proves to be without foundation. [11]

In 1775 Wesley wrote a letter to a nobleman, "I am an High Churchman, the son of a High Churchman, bred from the childhood in the highest notions of passive obedience and non-resistance." When we know some of the things that Wesley did, such as sending out lay preachers into recognized parishes of the Church of England and ordaining clergy, we are left a bit confused. Wesley, however, apparently had no problem with this apparent contradiction and seemed to sincerely believe what he wrote.

John and Charles Wesley between them wrote 162 Communion hymns. Charles wrote the majority of those hymns. The 1939 Methodist Hymnal contained eight communion hymns not one written by either of the Wesleys! The 1989 United Methodist hymnal contained only one Wesley hymn listed in the Communion Hymn section of the index. The hymn numbered 699, a Wesley hymn, was for some reason, not listed with the Communion Hymns, though it is obviously a Communion Hymn.

This neglect of the Wesley Communion Hymns is a serious omission, since like many Wesley hymns, they were written partly to teach theology, the theology of the Sacrament. The hymn mentioned above, number 699, speaks to the real presence of Christ in the Sacrament in a more agreeable way than does John M. Moore, mentioned a page or two back. The third verse says it more clearly:

Jesus, dear expected Guest,
Thou art bidden to the feast:
For thy self our hearts prepare;

Come, and sit, and banquet there. [12]

What can this be, other than an invitation to Jesus, to be present with us in Holy Communion? In J. Earnest Rattenbury's wonderful book, *The Eucharistic Hymns of John and Charles Wesley*, he shows us all 162 of the Wesley's Communion Hymns with commentary. Number 75 in the third verse says this:

Spirit of Faith, come down,
Thy seal with power set to,
The banquet by Thy presence crown
And prove the record true. [13]

One does not need to be a trained theologian to understand that the Wesley's believed that Jesus could be present with us at the Lord's Table, a real presence. There is no magic here as John M. Moore suggested, no superstition, no sacerdotalism. It is only hungry hearts, gathered around his table, opening those hearts to the presence of Jesus Christ. He can, and will, if asked, be present with us in a unique way, in the consecrated bread and wine, as we gather around his feast with open hearts.

In his sermon, *The Means of Grace*, Wesley lists the means of grace:

The chief of these means of grace are prayer, whether in secret or with the great congregation; searching the scriptures; (which implies reading, hearing, and meditation thereon;)

and receiving the Lord's Supper, eating bread, drinking wine in remembrance of him: And these we believe to be ordained of God, as the ordinary channels of conveying his grace to the souls of men. [14]

This is no mere memorial; it is God, through the ordained sacraments, interacting in love with human hearts. A little further along in that same sermon Wesley wrote as follows:

By "means of grace" I understand outward signs, words or actions, ordained of God, and appointed for this end, to be the ordinary channels whereby he might convey to men, preventing, justifying, and sanctifying grace. [15]

This quote demonstrates the enormous efficacy Wesley saw at work in the sacraments, especially in the Lord's Supper, in which God even dispenses salvation. These, and many passages that could be cited, leave no doubt that Wesley believed that God, in Christ, was truly present with humans in the Lord's Supper to the great benefit of humans.

In closing this section on Holy Communion, we can cite one more of the Wesley eucharistic hymns, to finally answer the question, "Did Wesley believe in the real presence of Christ in the Lord's Supper?

We need not go up to heaven, to bring the long sought Savior down; Thou art to all already given, Thou dost even now The banquet crown; To every faithful soul appear, and show Thy real presence here! [16]

Concerning baptism, Wesley, as he did in all doctrinal matters, adhered to the Articles of Religion of the Church of England. With "little Alteration" Wesley passed these Articles of Religion onto the American Methodists. The article of baptism was given to the American Methodists verbatim:

Baptism is not only a sign of profession, and mark of difference, whereby Christians are distinguished from others that are not baptized; but it is a sign of regeneration or the new birth. The baptism of young children is to be retained in the church. [17]

John Wesley contributes to some confusion at this point, since he also speaks of the new birth as that which comes to those who accept justification by grace through faith. In his sermon titled, *Marks of the New Birth*, he frequently speaks of being born of God. What, then, is the regeneration and new birth that comes with the baptism of infants and young children? For Wesley, the child, who has committed no sin, still possesses a sinful nature, inherited from Adam through the fall. That sinful nature is what is cleansed at infant baptism. Since people can fall away, the child at the age of accountability must make his or her own commitment to Christ.

Wesley in his, *A Treatise on Baptism*, explains his position. In that paper he tells us what baptism is, "It is the initiatory sacrament which enters us into covenant with God. It was instituted by Christ, who alone has the power to institute a proper sacrament, a sign, seal, pledge, and means of grace, perpetually obligatory on all Christians." [18]

In that treatise Wesley, speaking in defense of infant baptism, equated it with circumcision for the Jewish infant, one the old covenant, the other the new covenant. In stating the benefits to be bestowed in baptism, Wesley, lists several, the first being " And the first of these is the washing away the guilt of original sin, by the merits of Christ's death.[19] Then he listed several more benefits resulting from baptism other than the washing away of original sin. Second, "By baptism we enter into covenant with God". Third, "By Baptism we are admitted into the church, and consequently made members of Christ, its Head." Fourth, "By baptism, we who were, ' by nature children of wrath' are made the children of God." Fifth, "In consequence of our being made children of God, we are heirs of the kingdom of heaven." [20]

There is much about the sacraments that must remain a mystery to us. We accept the benefits by faith. In the hands of the uneducated clergy of the frontier, the theology around the sacraments was pretty much ignored. The questions about baptism came down to: Should infants be baptized and what was the proper mode of baptism, sprinkling, pouring or dipping? The unfortunate result was that both sacraments were stripped of their real meaning. The resulting lack of appreciation for the sacraments permeated American Methodism for generations. Thank God, we are beginning to recapture Wesley's theology of the sacraments.

CHAPTER EIGHT:
CAMP MEETINGS AND REVIVALS

I n the first chapter of this book it was stated that the camp meeting/revival movement of the nineteenth century, was one of the four factors that impacted on John Wesley's theology, which molded it into something quite different. Revivalism as defined by, *Webster's New Word Dictionary, Second College Edition*, 1970 is as follows: "e. a stirring up of religious faith among those who have been indifferent, usually by fervid evangelistic preaching." It would be difficult to come up with a better definition.

The first great revival on American soil took place largely among the Calvinistic Puritans of New England in the eighteenth century. The Rev. Jonathan Edwards, the scholar/pastor and apologist for Calvinism, played a dominant role in this sweeping revival that came to be known as "The Great Awakening".

George Whitfield, John Wesley's sometimes friend, crossed the Atlantic Ocean to be involved in the Great Awakening, and to move it from New England into the mid-Atlantic colonies. Wesley and Whitfield were soon to part company over the Calvinistic/Arminianism divide. Wesley was a strong defender of Arminian theology. They argued rather bitterly in print, and in letters they wrote to their respective friends. Wesley and Whitfield later reconciled and agreed to disagree theologically. Wesley preached Whitfield's funeral sermon.

Close to the end of the eighteenth century another revival movement began in the Mid-Atlantic States. It came to be known, as the "Second Great Awakening". This revival was not the work of scholars, such as Jonathan Edwards. It was largely in the hands of uneducated preachers. It was accompanied by new and strange physical and emotional manifestations.

As people began moving into Kentucky and Tennessee the revival moved with them and preachers on horseback kept the revival fires fanned. The closer to the frontier, the more pronounced the emotional and physical manifestations.

The camp meeting needs no other definition than the one given for revivals, "the stirring up of religious faith among the indifferent by fervent evangelistic preaching".

Once the revival left settled communities with concentrations of population and moved westward onto the sparsely settled frontier, it seemed a great economy of time and effort to bring people far and wide to the preachers rather than the preachers to the scattered settlers. This does not mean that the preachers did not go to the people when camp meetings were not going on; indeed, they traveled tirelessly bringing the Gospel to lonely cabins and remote settlements.

Bernard A Weisberger, in his book, *They Gathered at the River*, quoted a Presbyterian minister as saying, "Ambitious to find a family whose cabin had not been entered by a Methodist preacher, in several days I traveled from settlement to settlement...but into every hovel I entered I learned the Methodist missionary had been there before me." [1] These circuit riding preachers were everywhere on the frontier. A saying that was common on the frontier when blizzards howled and freezing rain fell was," Nobody will be out in this weather but crows and Methodist preachers."

Apparently, the crowds that attended the camp meetings came from many miles around in great numbers and they came to stay. The Rev. Henry Boehm, writing in his book, *Reminiscences of Rev. Henry Boehm*, describes a camp meeting in which he was involved.

Sabbath was a high day in Zion. There were about ten thousand people on the ground. In the morning Samuel Coate preached on John 3:17; and brother Ridgeway at night. One hundred and ninety-eight were converted and one hundred and sixty sanctified. Halleluiah! [2]

A little farther along he wrote of his own preaching on the next night.

> I preached at night on Luke xiv, 'And yet there is still room.' The work went on gloriously all night. During the meeting (the entire camp meeting) there were reported one thousand three hundred conversions and nine hundred and sixteen sanctifications.[3]

These figures are staggering, yet we have no reason to doubt the veracity of these traveling preachers. Certainly all camp meetings were not that large. One wonders where all these people came from. Frontier life could be very lonely. Camp meetings were great social events as well as religious events. Frontier families, who rarely saw anyone outside the family, or if they were in a small settlement, anyone outside the settlement, did a great deal of socializing during the camp meetings. Marriageable age young people met and courtships were begun which often ended in fine Christian families, It was remarked by detractors that, "At camp meetings more souls were made than were saved." This was grossly unfair, yet it probably contained a grain of truth. The woodlands environment and emotionally charged atmosphere would have been conducive.

The lay out of the camp meetings is interesting. They usually took place in a clearing carved out of ancient forests. There was a large assembly area around which tents were pitched. Others slept in covered wagons or lean-tos. Families cooked over open fires. At night pine knot torches lighted the campgrounds. At the end of the assembly area there was a raised platform with a pulpit. The platform and pulpit were commonly referred to as the "stand". Very large camp meetings might have several preaching stands going at once.

To announce that a meeting was about to take place a trumpet was blown and the people gathered at the stand. There would be singing of hymns and gospel songs. Scripture would be read and then one of the several preachers present would preach in a "fervid evangelistic manner". The goal of the preaching was to convict people of their sins, to instill in them a desire to flee from the "wrath to come" and to lead them into a vital converting experience through faith in Jesus Christ as their Lord and Savior.

The power of God falling on the congregation was accompanied by, what to us would seem strange, even frightening, manifestations, such as the "jerks", people barking like dogs, and people falling to the ground in an unconscious state. This later was referred to as "being in the spirit". Rev. Peter Cartwright, the flamboyant Methodist Circuit rider, described the jerks in this manner:

> Just in the midst of our controversy on the subject of the powerful exercises among the people under preaching, a new exercise broke out among us, called the jerks, which was overwhelming in its effects upon the minds and bodies of the people. No matter if they were saints or sinners, they would be taken

under a warm song or sermon and seized with a convulsive jerking all over, which they could not by any possibility avoid, and the more they resisted the more they jerked. If they would not strive against it and pray in good earnest, the jerking would usually abate. I have seen more than five hundred persons jerking at one time in my large congregations. Most usually persons taken with the jerks, to obtain relief as they said, would rise up and dance. Some would run, but they could not get away. Some would resist; on such the jerks were generally severe.

To see those proud young gentlemen and young ladies in their silks, jewelry, and prunella, from top to toe, taking the jerks, would often excite my risibilities. The first jerk or so, you would see their fine bonnets, caps and combs fly; and so sudden would be the jerking of the head that their long loose hair would crack almost as a wagoners whip. [4]

From what we know about John Wesley, we can assume, that he would have been quite uncomfortable with these strange manifestations of camp meeting religion. Actually, it is just about impossible to picture the proper little Oxford don in that setting. Yet, his pragmatism might have brought him to some accommodation, much as he accommodated to field preaching in the British Isles, a practice he found repugnant at first. The rationale for that accommodation to field preaching was, it worked, it won souls to Christ.

Explaining these strange actions, that accompanied camp meeting preaching, as merely emotional hysteria excited by fervent preaching, might cause us to miss something significant, namely, "God works in mysterious ways his wonders to perform."

We would find these manifestations repugnant and anyone acting in that fashion today would probably have several forced sessions with a psychiatrist. That behavior would only attract highly neurotic people to our churches. Yet who are we to say, that at a certain point in history, God could not have used methods we cannot understand.

Theologically speaking, the camp meetings blurred, for a short time, the theological differences between Calvinists and Arminians, so that they could work together to win souls for Christ in the highly emotionally charged atmosphere of American frontier religion. Would Calvin or Wesley have recognized their spiritual children in that setting? Probably not. The Presbyterian Church actually split for a period of time (1837-1869) over the emotional excesses of the camp meetings and revivals. The break was between the educated clergy of the east and the uneducated clergy of the frontier.

There was dissention over these matters in other denominations as well. As noted before, the Lutherans, Episcopalians, and of course, Roman Catholics were never involved in camp meetings and revivals. It is interesting to note that these churches held out for an educated clergy.

The Methodist Episcopal Church was the church most comfortable with the frontier camp meetings and revivals and the church that most profited from that approach. The "who so ever will, may come" approach of Methodism's Arminian theology made it a good fit for the frontier camp meetings and revivals. The camp meeting, though apparently, begun by Presbyterians in Kentucky with Methodist and Baptist participation, was more adaptable to Methodist theology. A theology which allowed people to choose to accept or reject God's offered salvation fit better with democratic principles than did a God who made all the decisions concerning human salvation. The frontier was populated by people of an anti-authoritarian bent. Methodists, at that time, came largely from the lower classes and were more comfortable with the emotional excesses of the camp meetings than were others.

The camp meeting was a great boon to Methodists, and was used by them longer than by others. Never the less, the camp meeting movement was short lived. By 1840 it had pretty much burned out. Its influence however was felt in American Protestantism long after the camp meetings ceased. There has been a great deal of nostalgia for the camp meeting in some circles. Here and there across the country camp meetings are still held, but they are vastly different from the frontier camp meetings.

What long term effect did the frontier camp meetings and revivals have on John Wesley's theology? The most noticeable effect was that it contributed to a highly individualistic approach to religion. The personal religious experience was made of utmost importance. To save one's soul and to escape the "wrath to come" was the consuming passion of religious experience on the frontier. In fairness it cannot be said that people converted in the camp meetings did not have a beneficial effect on communities in which they lived. They were a civilizing force on frontier life, which could use some civilizing. But the emphasis was on one's personal salvation, not on curing the ills of society, such as slavery. On the other hand, curing the ills of society was a strong emphasis of the Wesleyan revival in England. There, as we have seen, social issues, such as slavery, child labor, and prison reform were tackled by converts of the Wesleyan revival. Wesley did not allow for a separation between personal holiness and social holiness. One was meant to be busy ushering in the Kingdom of God.

Another impact of frontier religion on Wesley's theology can be seen in Wesley's doctrine of Christian perfection. As one reads the accounts of the early Methodist preachers concerning their experiences with camp meetings, one is amazed at the numbers of people who were converted and sanctified. One must wonder just what that sanctification was and how it related to Wesley's doctrine of Christian perfection. As was seen in chapter seven, for Wesley, perfect love, Christian perfection, sanctification, was inseparable from social ethics. The purpose of perfect love was to usher in the Kingdom we so often pray for when we say, "Thy kingdom come, thy will be done on earth as it is in heaven." The experience of sanctification for Wesley was not to make one feel good, not to give an emotional high, but rather to make one good, more Christ like, as one was governed by love for God and love for neighbor. According to Wesley the person who has perfect love will be busy at keeping the second commandment, loving neighbor as self. This will result in doing good to the neighbor (anyone in need) by all means possible. John Wesley and his followers were at the forefront of social reform in England.

The Christian perfection (sanctification) of the revival/camp meeting movement and the American holiness movement as taught by Phoebe Palmer and others was very much an esoteric, feel good experience, arrived at instantaneously by an act of faith.

Another impact of the camp meeting movement on Wesley's theology was what it did to Wesley's understanding of church and sacraments. Long after the camp meetings ceased, remnants of camp meeting worship, a completely free style with low regard for the sacraments, persisted in Methodist worship. Only recently has Methodism begun to return to Wesley's theology of church and sacraments.

Thousands of souls were saved at camp meetings. True many fell from grace and had to be saved again the following year and maybe the year after. These re-conversions were accompanied by the same physical manifestations as the first and provided the same entertainment for those who had come to be entertained. But many remained faithful to their religious faith. These became the leaven in the frontier society. They built churches in growing settlements. Soon there followed schools and courthouses. The impact of camp meetings was felt in American society for generations to come.

In spite of the strange manifestations of camp meetings, which would offend our modern sensibilities, it cannot be denied that God's convicting, saving and sanctifying grace brought many into a right relationship with God through Jesus Christ as Lord and Savior, and swelled the membership rolls of the Methodist Episcopal Church.

In the camp meeting movement God apparently used what God had available to accomplish God's purpose, the salvation of human souls, in a unique time and place. God did that once before, in ancient Palestine when he used twelve unlearned men, fresh from their trades, working outside the temple and synagogues, to bring his church into being, for that same purpose, the salvation of human souls.

CHAPTER NINE: FOUR FACTORS OF FRONTIER LIFE THAT IMPACTED ON WESLEY'S THEOLOGY TO CHANGE IT.

In the beginning of this book it was postulated that there were at least four factors of frontier life that impacted on John Wesley's theology to make it something quite different. The **First**, of these factors in importance was an uneducated clergy handling the rather sophisticated theology of the Oxford don; **Second**, was the plurality and proliferation of religious groups in America; **Third**, was the American mind set of the late eighteenth and nineteenth century, anti-intellectual and anti-authoritarian; And

Fourth, the camp meeting movement and frontier revivalism.

Now it is time to examine those four factors to see if the evidence put forth supports the premise of this book, namely that the American frontier changed John Wesley's theology.

American frontier religion, whether Methodist, Baptist, Presbyterian, or some of the newer movements born in America, shared some common characteristics. Frontier Protestantism was characterized by Biblical literalism, dispensationalism, revivalism, emotionalism and individualism. Holiness of an esoteric, individualistic, pneumatological nature was a part of much frontier religion as well. As we have seen, the holiness of the American Holiness Movement was a distortion of Wesley's doctrine of Christian perfection. Long after the frontier had come to a close, these characteristics of frontier religion, though in a somewhat tempered form, continued to mark American Protestantism.

The American frontier of the nineteenth century was a unique phenomenon. Nothing quite like it was ever seen before and nothing quite like it has ever been seen since. Most American denominations, were to some extent, at least, molded by frontier religion. The further we get from the frontier the less the impact of the frontier on religion. The more fundamentalist a church is, the more the impact of the frontier is still felt.

AN UNEDUCATED CLERGY:

Probably the most significant factor involved in the Americanization of John Wesley's theology on the American frontier was the lack of an educated clergy. On the American frontier there was, as evidenced by the writings of Peter Cartwright and others, an anti-intellectualism, an actual prejudice against educated clergy. In speaking of the Western Conference, which in 1820 and 1821 had been divided into the Ohio, Tennessee and Mississippi Conferences, Cartwright wrote:

> From the time I joined the traveling ranks in 1804 to 1820-21, a period of sixteen years, from thirty-two traveling preachers we had increased to two hundred and eighty; from eleven thousand, eight hundred and seventy-seven members, we had now over eighty-seven thousand; and there was not a single literary man (formally educated) among those traveling preachers. [1]

Cartwright gives us a good picture of how early frontier Methodist preachers were trained. Writing of a time, early in his own ministry, sometime before 1810 he says:

> We had at this day no course of study prescribed as at the present; (1856) but William McKendree, afterward bishop, but then presiding elder, directed me to a proper course of reading and study. He selected

books for me, both literary and theological; and every quarterly visit he made he examined into my progress, and corrected my errors, if I had fallen into any. He delighted to instruct me in English grammar.

...and I believe that if presiding elders would do their duty in this way, it would be more advantageous than all the colleges and Bible institutes in the land; for then they could learn and practice every day

...the Presbyterians, and other Calvinistic branches of the Protestant Church, used to contend for an educated ministry, for pews, for instrumental music, for a congregational or stated salaried minister. The Methodists universally opposed these ideas; and the illiterate Methodist preachers set the world on fire, the American world at least, while they were lighting matches! [2]

Peter Cartwright may not have been entirely accurate in ascribing the rapid growth of Methodism on the American frontier in the nineteenth century to the fact that Methodist preachers were "illiterate", but the above quotes do serve to show the low regard in which frontier Methodists preachers held formal theological education. Cartwright may have had a nugget of truth in his evaluation of the situation. Men unencumbered with the intricacies of theological inquiry may have been freer to simply be pragmatic, to do what obviously worked, that which brought the masses to Christ and the Church.

Fortunately, not everyone shared Peter Cartwright's sentiments. Methodists were to become, before the nineteenth century ended, great builders of colleges, universities and theological seminaries. During the first third of the nineteenth century, however, what Peter Cartwright was describing in the above quotes was probably quite typical of the traveling Methodist clergy. It is not surprising, then, that while these men believed themselves to be true followers of John Wesley's theology, they did real violence to his theology.

Theologically astute or not, no one can ever say of these men, that they did not set a standard in courage, dedication, sacrifice, and a passion for Christ and the souls of their constituents, that in all likelihood, will never be seen again. Across the mountains and plains of America unmarked graves hold the bones of some of those blazing disciples, who burned out and were gone before they reached forty years of age. The life expectancy of an early Methodist circuit rider, was at one time, less than forty years. That Methodism has never set aside a day to remember and honor these men seems strange.

Pluralism on the American Frontier:

The second influence on the American frontier that tended to Americanize John Wesley's theology, was the existence of a number of denominations with their many theological thrusts. That pluralism was present in Colonial America, but to a much lesser extent. Theology in Colonial America was still pretty much in the hands of an educated clergy, some highly educated. There wasn't much competition between theologies and little or no amalgamation. On the frontier, however there was real competition for the sparse population. In the hands of theologically uneducated clergy, in all the Protestant groups, theologies, began to amalgamate into a sort of American folk religion. The camp meeting/revivalism fervor of the frontier brought everyone together in sort of a religious hodgepodge. That is not to say that particular doctrines were not contended for, such as in the clash between the Calvinism of the Baptists and Presbyterians and the Arminianism of the Methodists.

In John Wesley's England, Methodism was juxtaposed against only The Church of England and to a lesser extent the Puritans and Quakers. As has been stated, Wesley saw Methodist doctrine to be well within Anglicanism. In America, Methodism was on its own against a number of churches and movements and was to some extent molded by them.

Impassioned theological debate by theologically naïve clergy tended to distort Christian doctrine. The religious pluralism of the frontier in the nineteenth century was a very different crucible for theological formation than that of eighteenth century England with its more homogeneous religions climate.

THE FRONTIER MIND SET:

The American frontiersman was self reliant, independent, equalitarian and not very impressed with outside authority. Fredrick A. Norwood, in writing of these clergy, contrasting them with those who had earlier been sent from England says:

> These men, Native Americans all, viewed the Methodist movement from a different perspective. They were certainly not caught up in Tory loyalties. The whole issue of authority looked different to them. Moreover being bred in a revivalistic religious scene, they were freer in their attitudes toward formally organized ecclesiastical bodies. Not surprisingly, these differences created considerable tension from time to time. [3]

As Methodism moved into the nineteenth century and away from the eastern seaboard, the influence of English preachers trained by Wesley faded and the influence of men described by Norwood became more and more dominant. This certainly colored the religious scene on the frontier.

Formal education was scarce on the frontier for clergy and laity alike. Religion played a dominant roll in the lives of the people as one of the few outlets for their emotions. Camp meetings and revivals were great social events. The experience of "getting religion" was usually, as we saw in the last chapter, accompanied by great emotional drama. The physical manifestations of conversion, such as the jerks and barking like dogs and falling unconscious, were expected.

CAMP MEETING/REVIVALISM:

In the last chapter we examined the camp meeting, which was simply an efficient approach to evangelism, adapted to frontier life. We saw how revivalism on the frontier molded American Methodism into something John Wesley would have had difficulty identifying as his movement.

The revival of religion in colonial America in the 1740's, known as the "Great Awakening" was a Calvinistic revival. It was in the hands of learned men, such as Jonathan Edwards. The revival of the late eighteenth century was Arminian. It has been called the "Second Great Awakening". The revivalism that moved westward out of the thirteen original colonies was an extension of the "Second Great Awakening". This second awakening was not in the hands of learned men, most especially after it left the Eastern seaboard and moved into wilderness territory.

Fredrick A. Norwood finds a relationship between the romanticism of the New England intellectuals and the revivalism of the frontier. Actually they are both manifestations of the same thing, the romanticism and optimism of the American psyche at the time. Norwood writes:

> Romanticism found expression in the rather sophisticated intellectual movements associated with people like Thoreau, Irving, and Longfellow, and especially in New England transcendentalism. It also found expression in a more popular form of emotional religion which

led to mass revivals and the camp meeting. People, generally, would know nothing of literary and philosophical romanticism; but they knew from personal experience all about conversion. [4]

Whether revivals took place in the urban east or in the wilderness groves of the west, Methodism was caught up in, and marked by revivalism. The camp meeting, a distinctly American invention, has been well scrutinized by historians, sociologist, and even psychologists. A great volume of literature on the camp meeting exists. For the purpose of this study it is sufficient to say that, as an extreme form of revivalism, it exerted a strong influence in the molding of much of American Protestantism for at least seventy-five years.

Other denominations grew squeamish about the emotional excesses of the frontier camp meetings and abandoned them. Only the Methodists clung to the camp meeting until, finally it was almost exclusively a Methodist institution. One of the reasons that Methodism used the camp meeting longer than others was that it fit so well with the itinerate system. It worked better for the circuit rider than it did for the settled pastors of other churches.

Around the mid nineteenth century, signs of decline, in the camp meeting movement, could be seen even in Methodism. Books and pamphlets were written in an attempt to keep the movement alive. Camp meetings continued here and there out of nostalgia, but their clout as molders of American

Protestant theology was gone by the last quarter century. Norwood in writing of the decline of the camp meeting has this to say:

> The effect on individuals of the camp meeting, based so largely on emotional appeal, may have been impermanent. Many who were saved had to be saved all over again next year. The whole movement eventually fell into various stereotypes. Nevertheless, the camp meeting left its own permanent mark on Methodism, especially in the south. If some lost the marks of grace too easily, others retained deep convictions for the rest of their lives. Certainly, a church enlivened by camp meetings was not likely to suffer early senility. [5]

There is little question that revivalism, whether in the camp meeting or not, was a molder of American Protestantism, especially Methodism. The theology that grew out of revivalism was strong on God's grace. It was, however, simplistic and individualistic. It sought its authority, not in the doctrines of the church, but in the emotional impact of the moment. The purpose of this religion was not so much the "vital piety" that Wesley had hoped for in Methodism, as it was the personal emotional experience of the moment. Religion was reduced to feelings. It was to be several decades beyond the camp meeting period before a social conscience was to become a part of the religious experience for American Methodism as it had been for Wesley in eighteenth century Methodism in England.

Perhaps other influences of the American frontier could be sited that impacted on Wesley's theology to make it and its practice something Wesley would have been uncomfortable with, and in some instances might not even have recognized as his own. But the four influences put forth in this book seem the most obvious in their impact on Wesley's theology and the strongest in molding American Methodism in its first hundred years.

The most obvious American departure from Wesley's theology can be seen in the meaning of the sacraments and in their administration and in other matters of worship. The other departures from Wesley's theology that have been discussed in this book are more subtle to the casual observer but just as significant, especially in the doctrines of Grace and Christian perfection. As has been previously stated, those two doctrines, as taught by Wesley, if recaptured in American Methodism, could contribute significantly to renewal of the church.

CHAPTER TEN:
CONCLUDING
THOUGHTS

In the first chapter of this book it was postulated that a major cause for our shrinking membership, for our people running off to other churches or to no church at all, was our lack of any theological consensus. The fact that we cannot stand together and say, "We believe..." does not make for a healthy church. There is no core around which we can rally. When we stand for everything we stand for nothing. Pluralism as a theological stance, either in principle or practice, simply has not served the church well. We can, as we have done, remove any mention of pluralism from *The Book of Discipline*, but we seem unable or unwilling to remove it from our church.

This is not a plea for a dogmatic, unthinking approach to Christian doctrines. That approach has not served the church well either down through the ages. Certainly there is room for study and interpretation around doctrines, but there is no room for the discarding or ignoring of basic doctrines. There does need to be a common core of doctrines around which we can gather. The historic creeds of the church were once that core for us and still are for millions of Christians.

One should not have to advocate for basic honesty in the church. There of all places, it should be a given. And, yet we have a problem. In our United Methodist service of ordination the bishop asks those to be ordained, "Are you persuaded that the Holy Scriptures contain all truth required for eternal salvation through faith in Jesus Christ?" "Are you determined out of the same Holy Scriptures so to instruct the people committed to your charge that they may enter into eternal life?" Those to be ordained answer, "I am so persuaded and determined by God's grace." The bishop then asks, "Will you give faithful diligence to minister the doctrine of Christ, the Sacraments, and the discipline of the church, and in the spirit of Christ to defend the church against all doctrine contrary to God's Word?" The candidates for ordination answer, "I will do so by the help of the Lord."

These are solemn vows taken to God before a crowd of witnesses within the church. And yet, how often they are cavalierly ignored. There is some room, within the boundaries of those vows, for differing understandings of scripture and doctrine, but unless one can come to a personal reconciliation in one's own thinking to those scriptures and doctrines, and keep those vows taken at ordination one should, the name of honesty, recant those vows and stop drawing a paycheck from the church.

As we draw to a close of this book we need to ask a serious question. "Why does any of this matter?" It matters because Methodism matters less and less to more and more people. The once vital, growing movement that shaped societies for the better is now a shrinking, powerless institution, composed of barely Christian people. Thanks be to God, examples here and there, especially in the third world, can be cited to contradict that statement. But examples are few and far between. Our membership rolls that once were swelling are now in a steady and dangerous free fall. We Methodists, for the most part, are a dying and powerless breed in America.

There are some who support the belief that the Wesleyan revival saved England from going through a bloody revolution such as France went through in the eighteenth century. This might be an over statement of the situation. Eighteenth century England was a very different nation than eighteenth century France was. Yet there is an element of truth here; the Wesleyan revival did have a positive impact on British society. John Wesley Bready in his little book, Wesley and Democracy, has this to say about Lord Shaftsbury, at one time Prime Minister of England who spent his life and his fortune changing the lives of the working poor in England, passing legislation to stop child labor, to educate children, to cut hours from the work week, and of Wilberforce and Buxton who worked to abolish slavery in England:

The guiding political axiom of this prophet and statesman (Shaftsbury) was "What is morally right can never be politically wrong, and what is morally wrong can never be politically right." The work of Shaftsbury, Emancipator of Industrial England, following on that of Wilberforce and Buxton, Emancipators of The Empire slaves, laid the moral foundation for Britain's free and democratic institutions. All these reformers were spiritual sons of Wesley, and these is no understanding of their achievements aside from the Evangelical Revival that inspired them. [1]

America at the present time faces several social problems that need working on. Wouldn't it be wonderful if we had some statesmen in the mold of Lord Shaftsbury who loved God and his neighbors more than himself?

Methodism was a strong moral influence in eighteenth century England and a strong moral and civilizing force on the American frontier as well. Those who had their roots in the Wesleyan revival had at their disposal the power to change lives and societies on both sides of the Atlantic. Can anyone say that we have not lost something vital out of Methodism?

When this author was a young pastor starting out in the ministry, just over fifty years ago, there was a press section at Annual Conference. The newspapers in the vicinity of the Conference would send reporters. Those newspapers would publish each evening what they thought were the important matter voted on. Today no one, outside the church, and most people inside the church, knows or cares what we do in Conference. We have definitely lost most of our influence in society.

Most of us are too sophisticated for the emotional excesses of frontier religion, a religion that once worked so well. The frontier is long gone and we in the twenty-first century are a very different people in many respects. Frontier religion no longer speaks to us in a meaningful way. We need something new, or perhaps something very old, older than our American frontier. What we have been doing for the last fifty years has not been working very well. In this book we have considered that Wesley's theology as practiced on the frontier was a distortion of that theology. The United Methodist Church today is like Walton's Wonder, the marvelous machine with ten thousand moving parts, which does absolutely nothing but move its parts.

What would happen if we were to take seriously the Article of Religion that has come down to us from the Church of England via John Wesley, Article XIII in the Articles of Religion of the United Methodist Church which reads, "the visible Church of Christ is a congregation of faithful men (people) in which the true word of God is preached, and the sacraments duly administered, according to Christ's ordinances, in all those things that of necessity are required to the same."

It is very clear that in all of Wesley's writing on the subject of Holy Communion that when he said the Sacraments are to be duly administered that he meant Holy Communion was to be administered every Lord's day. In his introduction to The Sunday Service of the Methodists in North America, he wrote. "I also advise the elders to administer the Lord's Supper every Lord's day."

There is at the present time a movement to put Holy Communion back at the center of our worship. This is a spiritually healthy initiative. We need to recapture Wesley's reverence for and understanding of the Sacrament and the deep spirituality that can and should accompany it. It needs to be honestly faced that the Wesleyan revival in eighteenth century England was as much grounded in the spirituality of the Sacrament as it was in evangelical preaching. Wesley insisted on both foundations. He hit upon a working balance between the two, something that we have tended to lose sight of. Wesley never scheduled his preaching services so as to conflict with Holy Communion in the parish church. Under Wesley's guidance the early Methodists were expected to attend the parish church for Holy Communion every week.

Some of those who object to a weekly celebration of Holy Communion today seem to believe that it was a latter addition to Christian worship. History simply proves that belief erroneous. From the time of the apostles the celebration of the Lord's Supper was central to Christian worship. In the Book of Acts we find the first pattern for Christian worship.(Acts 2:42). "And they devoted themselves to the Apostles teachings and fellowship, to the breaking of bread and the prayers." That sentence tells us much. The teaching of the apostles' would be equivalent to our use of scripture. The breaking of bread indicates the remembrance of the Lord's Supper. The article "the" before prayers would seem to indicate that there were set prayers to be used with the Lord's Supper.

Some will say that the breaking of bread simply means they ate together. In I Corinthians we find Paul writing, "The cup of blessing that we bless, is it not a participation in the blood of Christ? The bread which we break, is it not a participation in the body of Christ?" (I Cor. 10:16)

In the eleventh chapter of I Corinthians we find Paul giving some elaboration on the observance of Holy Communion.

When you meet together, is it not the Lord's Supper that you eat – for I received from the Lord what I also deliver to you, that the Lord Jesus on the night when He was betrayed took bread, and when he had given thanks, he broke it and said "This is my body which is for you. Do this in remembrance of me. In the same way also the cup, after supper, saying, "This is the new covenant in my blood. Do this as often as you drink it, in remembrance of me", for as often as you eat this bread and drink the cup, you proclaim the Lord's death until he comes – so then my brethren, when you come together to eat, wait for one another – if any man is hungry let him eat at home. (I Cor 11:23-26)

These passages from among the earliest Christian writings give evidence that when Christians gathered together, from the very beginning, the Lord's Supper was central to their worship and that it was not just a common meal. As Paul said, "If anyone is hungry, let him eat at home." "What, have you not houses to eat and drink in?"

In Justin Martyr's *First Apology*, a defense of Christianity addressed to the pagan Roman Emperor, Antonius Pius, he describes a Christian worship service. This comes from 140 A.D., It is too lengthy to include here, but the major parts of the service are not much different than present day worship when Holy Communion is observed. By this time about seventy year after Paul's death the pattern of Christian worship was pretty well set. Worship was conducted by a president. (presbuteros in Greek) In Methodist usage presbuteros translates in to fully ordained elders. Deacons distributed the bread and wine to those assembled. The deacons later took the bread and wine to those unable to attend worship. The writings of the Apostles were read and a homily preached. Prayers were said with the people standing. An offering was taken to aid the poor, widows and orphans. For those who doubt the centrality of the Lord's Supper in the church from the very earliest; evidence does not support their doubt. The evidence supports the fact that the Lord's Supper was not a later addition to Christian worship but that it was the central piece of Christian worship from the very beginning.

When we return to our roots and move toward a weekly celebration of Holy Communion, some will say, "If it is done too often it will lose its impact." Some people will say such things because our pastors have not been faithful in teaching what the sacrament is in Wesleyan theology, and what it does in us, and to us, and for us. Unfortunately some people will resist the attempt to recapture the centrality of Holy Communion because some of our pastors do not know what the Sacrament means in Wesleyan theology and what it can do spiritually for the communicant. Those pastors should pray for forgiveness and begin a serious study of the matter, beginning with Wesley's words on the subject and progress to the study of *This Holy Mystery*, approved for study in our church.

For Wesley, as we have seen, holy Communion was a sacrament in which Christ is truly present, a means of grace in which God, who is love, interacts with us in a loving relationship which changes us in to loving people, able to keep the two great commandments, love of God and love of others. If that sort of love became the norm in our churches, church renewal would take a mighty leap forward. We would be so attractive to those outside the church they would want in. We definitely need to recapture Wesley's sacramental theology; we need to understand the deep spirituality that accompanies the Lord's Supper.

The Sacrament, as a means of grace, according to Wesley, was not only for those within the community of faith, but also as a means of bringing those outside the church into a converting experience. Charles Wesley wrote in his communion hymn, numbered 339 in The United Methodist Hymnal, "Come sinners to the feast: let every soul be Jesus' guest. Ye need not be left behind, for God hath bid all human kind." What a beautiful and open invitation to come into a personal, vital loving relationship with God, through Jesus Christ as Lord and Savior.

In his Journal, Vol. Two, Wesley wrote:

"What is to be inferred from this undeniable fact – one that had not faith received it at the Lord's Supper? Why: (1.) There are means of grace – that is, outward ordinances – whereby the inward grace of god is ordinarily conveyed to man, whereby the faith is conveyed to them who before had it not: (2.) That one of these means of grace is the Lord's Supper: and that who had not faith ought to wait for it in the use of the Lord's Supper and other means of grace which God hath ordained. [2]

In his sermon, *The Duty of Constant Communion*, Wesley wrote, "This is the case: God offers you one of the greatest mercies on this side of heaven, and commands you to accept it. Why do you not accept this mercy, in obedience to his command? [3]

From these quotes it is apparent that Wesley saw Holy Communion as a means of evangelism, of bringing people into an experience of saving grace, into a relationship with Jesus Christ as Lord and Savior. This is something our churches definitely need. What would happen if we, with open arms would say to those outside the church, "The table is set, the feast is spread, come into the gospel feast, the feast of God's gracious love?" It might be that the harvest would be great.

We have seen that in his doctrine of grace, Wesley became a partial bridge between Calvinism with its emphasis on God's sovereignty to the exclusion of any human involvement in salvation and Arminianism which made human will primary importance in either accepting or rejection God's proffered love. Wesley, rather than coming down on either side of that dived, made it a matter of God's free grace. We have seen that Wesley's doctrine of grace, as a bridge between the two extremes was, was a casualty of the American frontier.

We have also seen that for Wesley, grace was not an entity, not a thing which God bestows on us. God's grace is God's love, God's very nature, God's personality interacting with our personalities in a loving relationship. If we offered this, might we not find takers in this world of ours, so desperately in need of love and acceptance? Could any board or agency come up with a better approach to evangelism? Could any study devise a better plan?

Very few of us are ready to go back to preaching a "hell fire and brimstone, be saved or be damned" religion. Even if we were so inclined we would not find a receptive hearing in this twenty-first century. The frontier is gone for good. But human hearts still hunger for something beyond themselves, something they crave but cannot define. People are running off after all kinds of craziness to fill that deeply felt spiritual need, even to reviving ancient heresies. And, all the time we, the church, have what they need to fill the void in their lives, a loving and accepting relationship with the God who is love, through Jesus Christ as Lord and Savior. If we could individually and collectively, as the church, model that relationship, and preach its availability from our pulpits, perhaps God could use Methodism again as in the past.

When pressed for a definition of Christian perfection, Wesley always fell back on the great commandment and the one like unto it, loving God with our whole beings and others as ourselves. If we were to strip away all the controversy and confusion that have clustered around Wesley's doctrine of Christian perfection and fall back on Wesley's (and Jesus') original doctrine in all of its simplicity and beauty, loving God and neighbor, we might well have that which could save the church in our generation.

Perhaps the word, perfect, on Wesley's part was a poor choice. One might question whether there are degrees of perfection, can something be more perfect or less perfect than perfect? Plato weighed in on that question. For Plato only the idea is perfect; reality is a flawed image of the idea. Never-the-less perfection can be a goal toward which we strive.

True, Jesus did say, "You, therefore, must be perfect, as your heavenly Father is perfect." (Math. 5:48) To make any sense that verse must be kept in context. Jesus had been talking about the inclusiveness of God's love for the righteous and the unrighteous. Hyperbole is a useful teaching method, which

Jesus used on several occasions. A camel going through the eye of a needle is a prime example.

Hyperbole may be a useful teaching method but it has the possibility for great mischief when taken literally. Has this been the case with the term Christian perfection? As one examines some of the holiness sects it would seem so. Perhaps a better term would have been perfect intentions. Perfect intentions, is certainly within the realm of possibility for the sincere Christian. The sincere Christian can intend to be like Christ in daily life and can work and pray toward that end, while trusting in the grace of God. Nevertheless, we are stuck with Wesley's term, Christian perfection, with all of its qualifying statements. When, however, through careful examination, we come to understand what Wesley was teaching in his doctrine of Christian perfection, we come to believe that it is a doctrine of great worth to all Christians on their spiritual journeys; something much needed in the church in our day.

The Rev. John Fletcher, a contemporary of the Wesley brothers, and Methodism's first systematic theologian, wrote in the first volume of his four volumes, *The Works of the Rev. John Fletcher, Late Vicar of Madeley*, concerning Wesley's doctrine of Christian perfection:

> What after all, is the perfection Mr. Wesley contends for...that is loving God with all our hearts and our neighbor as ourselves...It is but perfect love shed abroad in our hearts by the Holy Ghost given to us, making us, stead-

fast, immovable, always abounding in the work of the Lord. 4

If we who are barely Christian could pray for and submit to being governed by that kind of love in our lives and in our churches, it might be remarked of us as it was of early Christians, "Behold, how they love one another." If that could be said of us, would we not be attractive to those outside the church?

Then perhaps we could agree with Albert Outler, that great scholar of Wesley, when he said"

I've come to believe that he's got something we all need...this vision of the Christian life (complex in many ways, yet simple at its core) might help us toward that renewal of the church which we keep talking about and praying for and are yet denied because of our partisan confusions. 5

Will we be perfect? Certainly not in the sense that we will be without flaws. But as Wesley taught we can have prefect intentions. With St. Paul we can say, "Forgetting what lies behind we press on toward the goal of the prize of the upward of God in Christ Jesus." (Phil. 3:13-14) Will we fall short occasionally? There is probably no way out of that. But the good news is that God's grace, God's love for us, never fails even when we fail.

When Wesley's doctrine of Christian perfection is stripped of all the controversy, all the excessive claims made for it, stripped of all the wild emotionalism attached to it in the American holiness movement and in the camp meetings and revivals of the frontier, and restored to its simple, yet profound definition, that of loving God completely and our neighbors as ourselves, we just might have what could save the church in our generation. After all it's what Jesus commanded, "This is my commandment, that you love on another as I have loved you." (John 15:12) That would be perfect love, would it not?

NOTES

CHAPTER ONE

1. *Webster's New World Dictionary, second edition*, The World publishing Company, 1986
2. John Wesley, *The Works of John Wesley*, Vol. 1., Zondervan Publishing Company, Grand Rapids, Michigan. p. 31
3. Ibid. p. 31
4. Ibid. p. 31
5. Ibid. pp. 50-51
6. Ibid. p. 56
7. John Wesley, *The Sunday Service of the Methodists in America, (with an introduction and commentary by James White)* OSL Publications, Cleveland, Ohio, 1991. p. i Used by Permission
8. Ibid. p. iii

9. Peter Cartwright, The *Autobiography of Peter Cartwright: The Backwoods Preacher*, ed. by W.P. Strictland, Jennings and Graham, Cincinnati, Ohio, Eaton and Mains, New York, 1886. p. 4
10. John Wesley, *The Works of John Wesley*, Vol. VIII, p. 315
11. Sydney E. Ahlstrom, *A Religious History of the American People* (New Haven and London: Yale University Press, 1972) p. 746 used b y permission
12. John Wesley, *The Sunday Service of the Methodists in North America*, OSL Publications, Cleveland, Ohio, P. 1 used by permission

CHAPTER TWO

1. Albert Outler, ed., *John Wesley*, (New York: Oxford University Press, 1964) p.120 used by permission
2. John Wesley, *The Works of John Wesley*, Vol. 8, p. 46
3. Robert Tuttle, *John Wesley: His life and His Theology*, (Grand Rapids, Michigan: Zondervan Publishing House, 1978. P. 71 used by permission
4. Ibid. p. 73
5 John Wesley, *The Works of John Wesley*, Vol. 1., p. 224
6. Ibid. p. 262
7. Ibid. p. 450

8. Fredrick A. Norwood, *The Story of American Methodism*, Nashville: Abingdon. 1974, p. 42. used by permission

9. John Wesley, *The Works of John Wesley*, Vol. 8, p. 272

10. Howard Snyder, *The Radical Wesley*, (Downers Grove, Illinois: Inter Varsity Press, 1980) p. 68 used by permission

11. Albert Outler, ed. *John Wesley*, New York: Oxford University Press. 1964. p. 119

12. Ibid. p. 119

13. John Wesley, *The Works of John Wesley*, Vol. 8, p. 211

CHAPTER THREE

1. Mack B. Stokes, *The Bible in the Wesleyan Heritage*, (Nashville: Abingdon. 1979) p. 42

2. John Wesley, *The Works of John Wesley*, Vol. 6, p. 64

3. Ibid. p. 71

4. Ibid. pp. 65,66

5. Van A. Harvey, *A Handbook of theological Terms*, (New York: The McMillian Company 1966) p. 136

6. Albert Outler, ed., *John Wesley, Oxford Press, New York, 1964*, pp. 492, 493

CHAPTER FOUR

1. Mildred Bangs Wyncoop, *Wesleyan-Arminian Theology*, (Kansas City: Beacon Hill Press, 1967, p. 96
2. Ibid. p. 97
3. Ibid p. 99
4. John Wesley, *The Works of John Wesley*, Vol. 6, p. 57
5. Ibid. p. 510
6. Ibid. p. 512
7. Ibid. p. 509
8. Peter Cartwright, *Autobiography of Peter Cartwright: Backwoods Preacher*, (Cincinnati: Jennings and Graham) p. 218

CHAPTER FIVE

1. John Wesley, *The Works of john Wesley*, Vol. 11, p. 37
2. Ibid. Vol. 8, p. 131
3. Ibid. Vol. 6, p. 5
4. Ibid. p. 6
5. *The United Methodist Hymnal*, The United Methodist Publishing House, 1989. P. 384
6. John Wesley, The *Works of John Wesley*, Vol. 11, p. 374
7. Ibid. pp. 296, 297
8. Ibid. p. 369
9. Ibid. p. 366
10. Ibid. p. 367
11. Ibid. p. 367

12. Albert Outler, *Theology in the Wesleyan Spirit*, (Nashville: Discipleship Resources-Tidings. 1975) p. 71
13. Ibid. p. 71
14. John Wesley, *The Works of John Wesley*, Vol. 7, p. 205
15. Ibid. pp. 204, 206
16. Albert Outler, *Theology in the Wesleyan Spirit*, Disciples Resources, Nashville. P. 74
17. John Wesley, *The Works of John Wesley*, Vol. 9, p. 397
18. Ibid. p. 420
19. Ibid. Vol. 5, p. 126
20. Ibid. Vol. 11, p. 416
21. Ibid. p. 446
22. Ibid. Vol. 7, p. 136
23. Ibid. p. 138
24. Albert Outler, *Theology in the Spirit*, Discipleship Resources, Nashville, p. 80

CHAPTER SIX

1. John Wesley, *The Works of John Wesley*, Vol. 3, pp. 120, 121
2. Ibid. Vol. 12, p. 131
3. Ibid. p. 131
4. Ibid. p. 135
5. Ibid. p. 136
6. John L. Peters, *Christian Perfection and American Methodism*, (Nashville: Abingdon Press, 1983) p. 71

7. Thomas A. Langford, *Practical Divinity, Theology in the Wesleyan Tradition*, (Nashville: Abingdon Press, 1983) p. 51 used by permission
8. Ibid. p. 53
9. Ibid. p. 79
10. Peter Cartwright, *Autobiography of Peter Cartwright: Backwoods Preacher*, p. 24
11. Ibid. p. 25
12. Ibid. p. 130
13. John L. Peters, *Christian Perfection and American Methodism*, (Nashville: Abingdon Press. 1983) p.97
14. Ibid. p. 99
15. Ibid. p. 101
16. Ibid. p. 101
17. Ibid. p. 110
18. Much of the biographical material on Phoebe Palmer came from an article by Anne C. Loveland, Associate Professor of History at Louisiana State University, in the May 1977 issue of The Historian.

CHAPTER SEVEN

1. John Wesley, *The Works of John Wesley*, Vol. 14, p. 272
2. Wesley's introduction to, *The Sunday Service of the Methodists in North America*, OSL Publications, p. ii used by permission
3. Ibid. p. iii

4. John Wesley, *The Works of John Wesley*, Vol. 8, pp. 74, 75

5. Fredrick A Norwood, The *Story of American Methodism*, (Nashville: Abingdon Press, 1974) p. 121 used by permission

6. Ibid. p. 121

7. Ibid. p. 122

8. Ibid. p. 124

9. A. Raymond George, *The Sunday Service*, Doxology, OSL Publications, January 1984, pp. 5-13 used by permission

10. John M. Moore, *Methodism in Belief and Action*, Abingdon-Cokesbury Press, New York-Nashville, 1956. pp. 176-178 used by permission

11. J. Earnest Rattenbury, *Wesley's Legacy in the World*, Epworth Press, England, p. 63

12. *The United Methodist Hymnal*, United Methodist Publishing House, Nashville. Number 699

13. J. Earnest Rattenbury, *The Eucharistic Hymns of John and Charles Wesley*, OSL Publications, 1990. No. 75 used by permission

14. John Wesley, *The Works of John Wesley*, Vol. 5, p. 185

15. Ibid. p. 187

16. J. Earnest Rattenbury, *The Eucharistic Hymns of John and Charles Wesley*, OSL Publications, 1990, No. 75 used by permission

17. John Wesley, *The Sunday Service of the Methodists in North America*, p. 312
18. John Wesley, *The Works of John Wesley*, Vol. 10, p. 188
19. Ibid. Vol. 10, p. 190

CHAPTER EIGHT

1. Bernard A. Weisberger, *They Gathered at the River. Little*, Brown & Company, Canada, 1958, pp. 45, 46
2. Henry Boehm, *Reminiscences of Rev. Henry Boehm*, Nelson and Philips, New York, 1875, p. 150
3. Ibid. p. 150
4. Peter Cartwright, *Autobiography of Peter Cartwright*, Eaton and Mains, New York, 1856. pp. 48, 49

CHAPER NINE

1. Peter Cartwright, *Autobiography of Peter Cartwright*, Eaton and Mains, New York. p. 197
2. Ibid. pp. 78, 79
3. Fredrick A. Norwood, *The Story of American Methodism*, (Nashville: Abingdon Press, 1974) p. 80 used by permission
4. Ibid. p. 156
5. Ibid. p. 163

CHAPTER TEN

1. John Wesley Bready, *Wesley and Democracy*, The Thorn Press, Toronto, 1939, p. 54
2. John Wesley, *The Journal of John Wesley.* 8 Vol., Standard Edition, Nehemiah Cornock, ed. New York, Eaton and Mains, 1909, Vol. 2, p. 315
3. John Wesley, *The Works of John Wesley*, Vol. 7, p. 151
4. John Fletcher, *The Works of John Fletcher*, 4 Vols., Vol. 1, p. 270
5. Albert Outler, *Theology in the Wesleyan Spirit*, (Nashville: Discipleship Resources 1975 p. 80

BIBLIOGRAPHY

Ahlstrom, Sydney E., A *Religious History of the American People*, New Haven & London: Yale University Press, 1972

Bangs-Wynkoop, Mildred, *Wesley-Arminian Theology*, Beacon Hill Press, Kansas City, Missouri: 1976

Boehm, Henry, *Reminiscences*, Nelson & Philips, New York: 1875

Bready, John Wesley, *Wesley and Democracy*, The Thorn Press, Toronto, 1939

Cartwright, Peter, *Autobiography of Peter Cartwright*, Jennings & Grahm, 1856

Cox, Leo George, *John Wesley's Concept of Perfection*, Beacon Hill Press, Kansas City, Missouri: 1964

Fletcher, John, *Works of john Fletcher*, Four Vols. Schmul Publishers, 1974, (original 1770)

Harvey, Van A., *A Handbook of Theological Terms*, The Macmillian Company, 1966

Langford, Thomas A., Practical *Divinity, Theology in the Wesleyan Tradition*, Abington Press, Nashville. 1956

Mickey, Paul A., *Essentials of Wesleyan Theology*, Zondervan, Grand Rapids, 1980

Moore, John M., *Methodism in Belief and Action*, Abingdon-Cokesbury Press, New York-Nashville, 1956
Norwood, Fredrick A., *The Story of American Methodism*, Abingdon Press, 1974

Outler, Albert, Theology *in the Wesleyan Spirit*, Nashville: Disciples Resource-Tidings 1964

Outler, Albert, ed. *John Wesley*, New York: Oxford University Press, 1964

Peters, John L., *Christian Perfection and American Methodism*, New York and Nashville: Abingdon Press, 1956

Stevens, Abel, *A Compendious History of American Methodism*, New York: Eaton & Mains, 1884

Wesley, John, *Sunday Service of the Methodists in North America*, Order of Saint Luke Publications

Wesley, John, *The Works of John Wesley*, 14 Vols., Grand Rapids, Michigan: Zondervan Publishing House, 1975

Rattenbury, J. Ernest, *The Eucharistic Hymns of John and Charles Wesley*, O.S.L. Publications, Cleveland, Ohio. 1990

Rattenbury, J. Ernest, *Wesley's Legacy in the World*, Epworth Press

JOURNALS

George, Raymond A., "The Sunday Service 1784" Doxology, Journal of The Order of St. Luke in the Methodist Church (Spring 1984)

Loveland, Anne C. "Domesticity and Religion in the Antebellum Period: The Career of Phoebe Palmer" The Historian (May 1977)

Printed in the United States
115100LV00001B/43-57/P